To Nette,
I pray this blesse.

Mona L. Black
6/12

You Can't Fall Off The Floor

Mona Lisa Black

iUniverse, Inc.
Bloomington

You Can't Fall Off The Floor

Most of the names in this book have been changed to protect the privacy of those who may be affected by the tone of this book.

iUniverse books may be ordered through booksellers or by contacting:

iUniverse
1663 Liberty Drive
Bloomington, IN 47403
www.iuniverse.com
1-800-Authors (1-800-288-4677)

Cover Model—Evadne Haye

ISBN: 978-1-4620-0811-7 (pbk)
ISBN: 978-1-4620-0812-4 (ebk)

Printed in the United States of America

iUniverse rev. date: 4/7/2011

Dedicated To:

Eric, Erica, Vandy (Christina), Andrea, McKayla, and Christopher
I want you to look back at my life and yours one day and know that what I went through and what you will go through will be for someone else deliverance some day. I love each of you, and I am so sorry that I have not been the greatest mother, but my love for you will endure forever.

Also,

I love you Mommy! Thank you for believing in me and sorry that I had to tell the "family business", but it was time for the secrets to die.
Michael, Calvin, Andre, Shannon, and my special angel Robin. I love all of you so much.

Contents

Foreword

There are no three steps to automatic success. There are no twelve step programs, no hypnotists, shrinks, medications, preachers, or teachers who will help you with life issues until you first identify those issues and admit that you need and want help.

For ages, men and women, great and unknown, have written countless self-help books. Some of these books have been based on a period of their lives that they felt was so powerful and profound it could teach someone else a lesson. Some were written as a result of research done on topics for which the world wanted ready information. My favorite books are the ones written by people who have never had experiences in the area about which they write as if they are an "expert"...you know the ones "How to Raise the Poor Black Man" written by Bob Smith (the white rich Yale graduate) or "The Plight of the Single Mother" written by Kathy (married with no children).

I am from the school of hard knocks, so the only way to reach me is by having something in common with me, and that means more than being another black woman. I am so much more than the color of my skin. I am not a superstar, but my life story could easily be turned into a made-for-TV movie.

Unbeknownst to me, this book has been writing itself for thirty nine years. It was implanted in my heart to write in a place of loneliness and homelessness sixteen years ago, but I was only released by God to write it in 2009. In fact, I can honestly say that I was basically forced to write it by God. I needed very little research for all of the information that I will share during your journey through my life. However, I have leaned on the Lord to provide guidance in the words to say and the stories that I will reveal to you in this book. No one really wants to put themselves on "Front Street", but if my testimony can somehow take root in the hearts of a young or old reader and bless them, then my job will have been made complete.

Well, I mentioned that it is hard to help someone if you cannot relate to them, so I guess I need to disclose who this book was really written for, and who it is not. This will weed out all the people that would be so bored reading a book that really was not written with them in mind. First, this book is not really for drug addicts, drug dealers, nor three time convicted felons (because I am sure they could be using their time to read some good law books), people that have always followed the right course in life (You know…the ones that graduated from school, went to college, worked in their career field, got married, bought a house, had children they planned for, and are currently living happily ever after). You don't need this book, because it would only make you upset to know that most people don't live like you. This book is not really for the self righteous, nor people that screamed holy, holy, holy from their mothers womb, because they would spend the majority of the book judging people like me that didn't know they had a holy bone in their body until God revealed it to me… very recently.

This book is definitely for people that have been talked about, lied on, lied to, hurt, misused, cast away, rejected, threatened, beaten, raped, and left for dead; people with low self esteem, the suicidal, depressed, hopeless, helpless, in poverty, on welfare, had-kids-out-of-wedlock, dated all the wrong men, had all the wrong friends, had-good-credit-then-bad-credit, loved-to-quickly, didn't-love-enough, been-married-then-divorced…oh, and for all the other people that don't know really where they fit in, but they just need something comforting to read.

This book is also a tribute to all the women who hoped against hope that they would have another meal for their little ones to eat, not considering their own next meal. And all the mothers and fathers that had children that did not come with instructions, but brought them home anyway and did the best they could to help them grow and caused least harm to their development, emotions, and spiritual well-being.

This book is a tribute to every girl that has ever wondered if she was actually taken home by the right family at birth. To those girls who are now women who were told they were too black, light, short, or tall, to those who were told they were too fat, ugly, and their hair was too short, stringy, curly, or nappy. To the mother who had babies and sacrificed their figures for 9 months, and never quite got back into the size 8 jeans after that. This book is for all of you.

I must admit there have been very few books that have been written for us… the not-so-prefect people. Books that let us know it's okay to not be perfect. So sit back, put your warm socks on, take off your "judgment hat," lean back in your chair and relax for a little while. Enjoy opening doors to the times in my life that I pray will heal you from the times in yours. Feel free to cry when you need to, and laugh all you want to, remembering always that… you can't fall off the floor.

CHAPTER 1

The Beginning Is Never the End

I must began by stating, a perfect little girl with blonde hair, blue eyes, two parents playing with me through the nursery window and looking at me as if I were a precious jewel, with a nursery full of items waiting to greet my birth and usher me into a picture perfect life is not who I was, or how life began for me.

My birth actually was clouded in mystery. My mother never told me if she was happy or sad the day I came into this world. There were no pictures that demonstrated their love for me on that special day. I do have enough sense to know that I was not a planned pregnancy. I reasoned this because how many black families really planned pregnancies in the 70's. I don't know if my father was at the hospital or even in the same city the day that I was born. Maybe he was sober, but most likely not.

My name is Mona Lisa, I was born May 15, 1970. I often thought that it had to be raining the day that I was born, because that would be the forecast for the most part of my life. I was born to common parents of a black community that was plagued with poverty. My mother was a nurse, my father, a jack-of-all-trades. I was never sure of what job my father had when I was born, or if he even had one. All my life he would leave every morning as if going to work, but would rarely bring money home to help support his six children. The one thing that I did know was that my mother worked. I know she worked because I never really remember her at home. She lived in her sterile white uniform all of my growing years. The only time she ever stayed home that I can remember is when she had my little sister, and she could not even enjoy that down time, because as I said, daddy went to work, but the money never quite made it home on Fridays.

Anyway, I always knew I was the opposite of everything my mother hoped for because if the truth be told she married my father because he was mixed with African American, white, and Indian. That was very important back then, because being dark skin back then automatically earned you a life of trouble and struggle. My mother is what you would call color struck. My father was fair skin, and she hoped that his light skin would overshadow her extremely smooth pretty dark skin, and bring to birth a light skinned baby… oh, don't forget with good hair, because you can't have a nappy headed light skin baby. That would go against everything that was considered beauty during the 60's, 70's, and 80's. I guess no one ever told my mother "the nurse" about genes! Well, I came into this world not only dark skinned, but with a bald head, that I would keep until about age 3. No wonder there are very few pictures of me before age 6 in my parents' home. I was the 5th child of 6 children born to the same parents. I would be considered an outcast today because my parents actually did the death do us part thing, and you see most African American children today don't even have a concept of what a marriage looks like.

The home that I came to was a two room apartment in the Marcy Projects of Brooklyn New York. There were no bells and whistles in this home. It was just a place to keep the rain and other elements from overtaking us, and store the little bit of stuff we had. The little that I remember about the home was that it was in great need of paint, and the elevator never worked, and we lived on the 10th floor.

My sister Sherry was very happy about my birth. As a matter of fact I know she was the only person that actually prayed to have me. Sherry already had one older brother, Mike, and two younger brothers, Donald and Ronald. So many times she desired a little sister to play and grow up with. She was 7 already when I was born, but she never minded carrying me on her little hips. Sherry had been very sickly as a baby, and even when I came home she was gripped with asthma and a very fragile body. My sister Nikki would come on the scene 4 years after me, but I don't think Sherry was as happy to see her…I know I wasn't.

They say that most kids don't remember things before age 2 or 3, but I beg to differ. I feel it depends on how much of an impact a memory has on your life will depend on how well you remember it. I wish that I could say that my earliest memory was sitting near the Christmas tree with loads of presents surrounded by my siblings, parents, extended family and friends; But my earliest memory happen when I was a little over 1 year old. We were still living in the two bedroom apartment. We had cats, and in the projects just like in a trailer park, all you have are wild cats who bring friends. I was very scared of them, and I still have a fear of them to this day because many days

I would wake up from a nap or in the morning and they would be licking the milk from my mouth and scratching my face. The scariest times were waking in the morning knowing my mother had left the bottle in my mouth to keep me sleeping, as she quietly darted down the stairs to walk my brothers to school; then I was attacked by cats for my food. Fighting wild cats is not fun for a 1 year old. I would wake crying and screaming, as I hugged the pillow for protection. Looking back on 39 years, it seems I have been fighting cats all my life.

I remember some mornings being in the bathroom on the sink watching my father shave. Like an artist with his work, my father would take great care in grooming himself. My father was so handsome that it didn't take much for him to look good. I just liked being in there with him because that was the only time I was able to get attention all by myself. Just that 10-15 minutes in the morning made me feel good, because even in my little, one year old mind I knew that for the rest of the day many of my cries would go unanswered, and my brothers, who always had each other to play with, would take pride in the hours of terror and teasing inflicted upon me. My mother would be too busy with the blows of life, or tired from working to concentrate on my little voice calling to her. At that point, during her down time from her two jobs she had five calling, needing and wanting kids, and one husband who was worse to deal with than any of the children.

Well, the first day of my true memory started the usual way. Daddy was shaving, and I was being a good student to all of his "teaching." He put the shaving cream on my face and used the back of the razor, pretending to shave me. I laughed because the back of the razor tickled. I also found joy in the way he smiled at me, and his hazel eyes shimmered in the dim light of the bathroom. After shaving class, I would trail at his heels into the kitchen. Though my father was not a chef, I remember him fixing pretty good meals for us. Meals we had to eat even if they were not appetizing because daddy did not believe in throwing food away. Not eating all your food in our house was like an Indian girl having sex before marriage. It was a sin, and it could get you hurt, if not beating to near death.

That "memory" morning was cream-of-wheat day. In most northern homes during that time, and even today the breakfast cereal was either oat meal, cold cereal (for black families, corn flakes, you would add your own sugar) or a bagel with jelly and cream cheese, or cream of wheat. I never remember grits and eggs before age 5. In fact, finding a bag of grits in Brooklyn was like finding a black woman at a hockey game. But I digress, after eating all of my breakfast I went in the living room to watch my morning shows, which were Sesame Street, Electric Company, and Zoom.

Just before lunch my 1 ½ year old mind was bored, and I found myself playing in the bathroom like most kids do. That is when daddy's black shaving bag caught my attention, somewhat like Eve looking at the tree in the Garden of Eden. It was calling me and enticing my little hands to touch it. I am not sure if I thought of calling Adam; who would have been my brother Ronald, and my faithful partner in crime, but I did not. There was no talking serpent on the floor, but something was telling me to just touch it. I was all alone with daddy's shaving bag and who would know? I had no idea that the next few moments were going to forever change my life, and how I viewed my father.

I jumped up on the toilet and then onto the sink to get a closer look. Then I put my hand into the bag and onto the black handle of the razor. This was no ordinary razor. It was an old-timey one that required you to replace the blade on your own. My father felt that no respectable man would use a disposable razor.

The moment it was out of the bag, I put it to my face as I had watched my daddy do countless times before. I didn't feel the danger. I guess being only 1 ½ years out of the womb was what made me fearless to most things. But I surely felt the danger when I heard my father's voice calling my name, and asking where I was, just as he walked into the bathroom. The dark look on his face sent chills up my spine, but that feeling was so short lived I never had time to enjoy it. He grabbed me by the arm, and cursed at me from the top of his lungs, I was not sure of all of the words he was saying at that time, but I would have a lifetime to learn the meanings to each word and hear them from his mouth on a regular basis. In addition, I felt the results of his displeasure. The beating that I got on that day from the man that I held as a hero and protector would heavily influence the issues that I would have growing up, and who I would become. How could my funny, handsome father be hitting me so hard? I was his favorite... or so I thought.

In those moments that seem to go on forever, I wondered where my mother was. Could she hear me screaming for my life? Could she hear this man teaching me "a lesson"? It was that day I learned that the people you expect to protect and love you will never come when you really need them, and sometimes the people that you live with will be just as scared as you are to face the abuser. However, you will always be expected to be strong enough to take "the lesson" that is given, and live to see another day.

I wish that I could say that child abuse was the only memory that I had but it was not. Because then writing this book would be pointless. I often times wondered why I did not remember much about my mother before I was 3 or 4, and the things that I did remember were not really good. I guess because my mother did not play a leading role in her own life story during this time. She was not even a supporting actress; she was much like an extra or walk on. I would not start seeing her name in the credits until I was too old to really care.

I remember seeing mom getting ready for work. My mom had the darkest, prettiest skin, and a smile that would put the Crest spokes-model to shame. She didn't need make-up, but when she put just a little on, she looked amazing. Behind the smile that she painted on each evening, before she ran off to work the night shift at an area hospital, there was a world of hurt, pain, and disappointment. It only took looking into her brown eyes to see that the lights that held hope had burned out.

My mom did not just live with her five kids, and husband, but she lived with this "pink elephant" I like to call my father's other side. You see, my father had a dark side of him that came out most days after noon, if we were lucky.

Daddy had been drinking since he was a teenager, and though he loved alcohol, it didn't like him and it changed the man that he could be. There are several types of drunks. The kind that drinks and become chatty, the kind that love to hug and tell you how much they love you, the drunks that get quiet and go to sleep, and the ones that cry and get depressed (like me). Unfortunately there are the ones that get mean as hell, the ones who want to fight, and the ones that will call you every SOB, MF, and other curse words that don't even go together… the latter at its most intense would describe my father.

Daddy never knew how to drink one beer, or one glass of vodka. If he got beer he had to drink the whole six pack…or case. And if he got a half gallon of vodka, you could be sure that he was going to drink it until it was either all gone, or he was passed out. By the time I was born, my father was what you would call a hopeless but functional drunk. When he had a job, he never allowed his problem to keep him from awakening by 5 a.m. and leaving the house by seven.

My mother, most times, would play his alcoholism down by not saying anything. I remember her lying to her friends many times when we would go see them. My mom's best friends "Sister" and "Brother" Harrison, seemed to have the perfect marriage, and my mom always wanted to pretend with Sister Harrison that my father was just as good a husband as hers. Therefore, on the very day we visited with them my father had choked my mother at the breakfast table for her voicing, "You don't do anything to help with the kids and these bills." When Sister Harrison asked her, "How is Edlee doing Marie?" Mom half smiled and said "Oh, he is fine…he is working today."

Although I was 3 at the time, I learned very quickly, in life never to let my thoughts exit my mouth. We had endured many slaps-in-the-mouth or extension cord beatings from speaking out-of-turn in our family, or telling "family business".

I just looked at my mom as she spoke to her best-friend wondering, who was "Edlee" they are talking about. Because, if it's my daddy Edlee, then we left him passed out drunk on the sofa before walking to her house. I think that my mother's best-friend knew that she was lying about my father, but as best-friends often do, she played along.

I knew very early in life that there was something very different about our family. Besides my father having the issue with his temper and alcoholism, we spent many days isolated. Even though our early years were spent in a city where we did not have many relatives, I never remember having family over at our house. I remember my mothers' friend, Sister Harrison had two sons (Eric and Kevin), and they were our only friends. They never came over to our house, but my mother would let us go to theirs sometimes. I knew that the only reason they could not come over was because she never knew what type of mood Daddy was going to be in from minute to minute. It seems however that the times we were allowed to go over there were always in the times of crisis.

Like when Daddy drank so much one day that he had an episode where he could not stop laughing and they took him to the mental hospital.

My mom gave my brothers and older sister "the talk" before the Harrison's came to get us… "You better not talk my business!" We went to the Harrison's and had to pretend that life was good. Daddy went into the hospital for a few days to detoxify, and my siblings and I were glad for the break.

Going in and out of the hospital to detoxify never stopped Daddy's behavior. My dad had been drinking heavy, chain smoking, cheating, and beating mom long before I came on the scene. I am sure my mother was depressed, and wished to hell that she would have listened to my Aunt Rebecca, who raised her in NY. She told my mom not to marry that man, but did she listen…no.

Mom needed to have faith in something to "escape" her terrible marriage, so one Saturday morning when these seemingly well dressed women appeared at our door, she began having private "bible studies" with them.

My sister Sherry spilled the beans one day while talking to my brother Mike about why we felt different from other kids growing up. It was because her life was somewhat normal up to the age of 6 or 7.

These seemingly innocent "bible studies" changed the way my mother thought. Before my older siblings knew what happen she jumped right into the "religion" called Jehovah's Witnesses and their lives as they knew it was over. My brother Ronald, me, and my sister Nikki were born into this cult, so we never knew better. I don't know how weak minded you have to be to find yourself the victim of a group such as this, but my mother was and to this day still a part of them. Sherry said that they were normal until this time right after Donald's 1st Christmas, so I am thinking about 1964.

For all who have no idea what I am talking about, let me give you a crash course in "Jehovah's Witnesses 101," and why just being a part of a religion such as this can be hell on earth for a child.

Jehovah's Witnesses are controlled by a "Governing Body" which they claim is the "faithful and discreet slave". Don't ask me what that means! This group consists of 10 to 15 mature men that, Jehovah's Witnesses are told, have direct guidance from God. The Governing Body, in turn, instructs followers with this guidance through the pages of the Watchtower and other publications. Jehovah's Witnesses are told by this "Governing Body" that Scripture alone is insufficient to understand the things of God. One needs the Watchtower Society and the literature it publishes to properly understand the Bible. Okay, so here we have someone telling you that the BIBLE is not enough...*GODS HOLY WORD...not enough? Seriously?*

The Society teaches that unless we are in touch with this channel of communication that God is using, we will not progress along the road to life, no matter how much Bible reading we do. They believe these are the instruments God is using to teach the world the deeper meanings of the scriptures. People are not to think for themselves but instead submit to the Watchtower Society's teachings.

Let's stop right here in the lesson. Okay, I am no bible scholar, and until recently I found it hard to read my bible for more than an hour a week, but somewhere in my bible I saw it written that we as individuals should "study to show thyself approved unto God." (2 Tim 2:15)

Jehovah's Witnesses believe they are the only people on earth that are serving God and the only ones that will be saved. One dare not question the teachings of the Watchtower Society; one who questions the Watchtower Society is considered to be weak in faith and could be "disfellowshipped."

Now being disfellowshipped is the equivalent of being told to get out of the church. Yep, you're not welcome because you did wrong. Do you ever think that you will ever hear T.D. Jakes, Creflo Dollar, or even your own pastor tell a member that they can't come to church, or that if they come to church no one can talk to them and they have to sit at the very back? That is crazy right? But it happens in this cult that masks itself as a religion all the time. As a matter of fact, my brother Lee, and sister Sherry would be turned in by my mother in their teen years to the cult leaders for "sinning." My brother smoked cigarettes and my sister Sherry went out with a boy that was not a Witness. Both of them were disfellowshipped. I know personally that both of them were so glad the day they got kicked out they could kiss the dirty ground and scream freeeeeeeedom!!!

Okay, then there is the list of all the things you can't do as a Witness. Jehovah's Witnesses are not allowed to salute the flag of any nation, recite the pledge of allegiance, stand for or sing the national anthem, run for public office, vote, or serve in the armed forces. Jehovah's Witnesses are not allowed to celebrate Christmas, birthdays, Easter, Thanksgiving, or any other holidays. So what! You were born on May 15? There is no reason to celebrate! Oh, and my personal favorite was always that Jesus was not born in December, so Christmas is a useless day. But then when I would ask, "Well why we can't celebrate Mother's Day, or Father's Day?" Then my mother would sharply reply… "Because the elders said we can't." Yep, that was the answer for most things with the Witnesses.

There is one topic which is at my top 10 things to ask God about when I get to Heaven. Okay, Okay, let me take this time right now to talk about the 144,000 "chosen ones". There are only 144,000 people, who are all Jehovah's Witnesses, which have ever been able to participate in the ceremony that other religions call communion. They have this ceremony about a week or two before we have Easter, and they just pass the cup and the bread all over the Kingdom Hall, but no one is allowed to drink or eat!

Okay the cock and bull story is that The Heavenly Kingdom took effect in 1914 with the invisible enthronement of Christ as King. A little flock or Anointed Class of about 135,300 people currently occupies it. All were selected after Christ's ascension into heaven at Pentecost (33 AD). During subsequent centuries, the selection of the full complement of 144,000 was completed in 1935. This fortunate group will spend eternity as spirit creatures in heaven with God and Christ and will rule over the other Jehovah's Witnesses who remain on earth. Those spending eternity on earth are what Jehovah's Witnesses call the Great Crowd or Other Sheep.

Now…come on people you don't see the sheer stupidity in this theory? First of all, God is God all by Himself. Why would He need to create 144,000 other gods to rule with Him? Now I know my father was not a well educated man, so I would expect him to fall for this, but my mom? She went to college! All I have to say is READ A BOOK! Nothing good can happen when people start creating their own bibles. Ask the people that followed Jim Jones the Peoples Temple leader who lead more than 900 people to commit suicide in 1978.

Oh, and Jehovah's Witnesses are not allowed to associate with non-Witnesses including family. Exceptions are made if the non-Witness family member is living in the same household. So I could talk to my daddy who could give a hoot about a Witness, or a victim for that matter! But my grand parents who lived in the same city with us and both my aunts that were there also, we could not even think about visiting. But this did explain why I don't remember any of my grandparents, aunts, uncles, most of my cousins, and why we had no friends. Yep, we were different for sure. I won't even bother to tell you all the rest of the things that Witnesses believe, because looking back now, it was and is just plain stupid. However, bookmark this page, because it will shed light on what would be the next 34 years of my life.

Oh, did I mention my father was an Atheist? So you are already getting a picture for where this story is going right?

CHAPTER 2

Secrets That Steal, Kill, and Destroy

Religion for many people is the rock of ages. It bonds families together. It bonds communities together also. But religion can also tear apart a whole family, and leave decades of hurt, bitterness, regret, and disaster.

Shortly after I was born, my grandmother Agnes died in Savannah, Ga. I was only three months old, so I don't remember her at all. Some of my siblings actually met her, before my mother got initiated into the cult. However, her life was cut short by ovarian cancer. My mother received the news that her mother had died from one of her sisters, or maybe even her Aunt Rebecca (we called her Sister. I think every black family has an Aunt Sister somewhere in it). I am sure that this was one of the only times that my daddy felt sorry for her, so he made a way for her to attend the funeral in Savannah.

My mother had two older brothers, and four younger sisters. My grandmother had been married to my mother's father, but after my mother came along he realized that he wanted to be free, so he got a divorce and moved to New York, leaving her with three kids. Well, when my grandmother remarried, the man she was with did not want her other kids, so my Aunt Sister who had no children took my mother and her two brothers to live with her in New York. My grandmother had four girls from her new husband and raised them in Garden City, Georgia.

My Mom came to Savannah to say goodbye to her mother. This was Aunt Rebecca's only sister, and only sibling left. As quiet as it was kept, my grand aunt had a brother that was mysteriously found dead way before I was born. My great grandmother Rosa Paige was still alive and kicking, and she would remain that way for another 19 years after the death of her daughter Agnes.

My mom was down there with all her family, driving to the church where they would sing many old Negro spirituals, say some prayers, and lay my grandmother to rest. However, before they could get all the way to the church my mother made the driver stop the car and pull over. When he did, she jumped out, and told all her siblings, aunts, grand mother, and other mourning, waiting family and friends that she could not go into the church.

Oh, yes she did! She said that it was against her religion to go into a church. All of her sisters tried to talk to her, and her aunt did to; but my mother was good and brainwashed by then, so I guess she thought that Charles Russell (the founder of Jehovah's Witnesses), was going to pop up all the way down in Savannah, Ga., spy her in that small church, and pull her membership. So she did not go into her own mothers' funeral service.

Now, this one act of religious loyalty caused a bomb to go off in this family and in Savannah that rivaled that of the planes hitting the building on 9/11. It was like the insult heard around the world.

In most black families they take death very seriously. I don't care if you were the trashiest of sinners, and you smoked weed, snorted cocaine, cursed, got killed while committing a robbery, and had sex with many different people down to your last second on earth. A sanctified preacher somewhere will find a way to squeeze you into heaven. Somehow, even people that commit suicide have a chance at heaven if you know the right preacher. Then at the burial, people will almost injure themselves not to walk on the surrounding graves, because they still have respect for the dead.

Oh, and everyone that knew you from birth is going to show up at the funeral. I don't care if they had not laid eyes on you in 40 years. When the word goes out that you are dead, somehow everything that you have ever done in life is forgiven, and you are a saint for a few days. In addition, if you are on this side of the dirt, and not in prison when your mother dies in a black family, you are expected to show up at the wake and the funeral. In fact, a black family will hold a body out of the ground up to three months (remember James Brown's dramatic wake?), just to make sure everyone who wants to be at the funeral is there.

Therefore, in the summer of 1970, for my mother to become a "hero" and fix her mouth to say that she came all the way from New York to Savannah, and refuse to go to her mothers' funeral because the Jehovah's Witnesses told her she could not go in a church or congregate with "worldly people" won her a free ticket to "black sheep-ville".

Now in the defense of black families everywhere, we tolerate a whole lot, and we forgive a whole lot. I mean we forgive murders, rapist, thieves, liars, Michael Jackson, Jessie Jackson, OJ Simpson (but not the last time, cause that was just plain stupid for him to rob that man), and now Tiger Woods; but there is no forgiveness for not going to your mom's funeral. So what happened you ask? Well, everyone from Savannah all the way up to New York turned on my mom. I mean the only people she had in her corner by 1971 was the cult, and us.

Though time has gone by, and some of the people that were alive during that time have gone on to be with the Lord, the stain of that day has still remained with this family. And, I think all of the ones that died wrote the story down and left it for their kids for future reference so my mother would never live it down and future generations would not make such a grave mistake. After that my mother plunged deeper into the cult, she really did not have to worry about her sisters much, because they cast her out like week-old fish heads. My Aunt Barbra is still the only one of her sisters to this very day that reaches out to her. The other ones have little to nothing to do with her, and it's really sad. Oh, and did I mention, that the good have to suffer with the bad? Because my mother did the unthinkable, the little victims in it all have had to suffer also. For this reason, there are still some cousins, and relatives that I have never laid my eyes on, and some of my aunts treat us like we are outcasts.

That is a perfect example of how religion can separate a family. However, I tell you that since I have been grown, I have seen other religions where mind-control groups function within it. I have even been a member of a church where the pastor became the "god". The members began to worship the pastor more than they worship God. But as soon as God allowed me to discern what was really going on, it was very easy for me to move right along. So my advice to all would be, learn to have a relationship with God for yourself. God will reveal himself to you by way of His Word, and no matter what happens in your religion never let it separate you from your family.

In 1974 my father was between jobs yet again, and he told my mother that he was going to Savannah to find work. He took the older kids with him; Ronald and I were left with my pregnant mother. During that time he was supposed to be living with my great grandmother. Somehow, Mom got word that he was not looking for a job at all, and that he was down there shacking-up with some woman or women. Needless to say, this was not a happy pregnancy for mom. I don't remember her smiling much during those months. However, my happiest times during that period were on the days when my mom had to go to the doctor. Ronald and I would be in tow as we walked through the streets of Brooklyn, caught trains, and enjoyed our adventure to the doctor's office for that day. We always knew that if we were good, my mom was going to take us to Burger King. We would have the opportunity to wear the King's crown (thank God that the elders never had a issue with kings, because we would have even missed those few times of joy and being a kid). Eating at a place where we never ate when daddy was here, made us feel so much better. You would have thought that we were eating steak in a five-star restaurant. It seems that just those few hours were the happiest of my life for a while.

Right after my sister Nikki was born, we boarded a plane to join our family in Savannah. By then, my father had found us an apartment in the projects of Savannah. Now the Marcy Projects were big, and yes you had crime and things like that, but the Hitch Village Projects of Savannah was a whole other thing. In New York you could find hard working people in the projects, and most of them would be considered middle class down in Savannah. Well, in Hitch Village there was a lot of no class, poor black people all around. Not everyone, but there were a great majority more people struggling, uneducated, fighting in the street, robbing, and selling dope than we were used to. I remember my father killing a rat outside our apartment that was as big as a cat. The roaches were not scared of people, and I was always too scared to turn on my light at night or get out of my bed to pee for fear that my floor would be covered with them. During our first two weeks living there, we went to the Kingdom Hall, and we got robbed for all of our stuff. Welcome to Savannah!

By this time my Aunt Sister had retired and moved back to Savannah also. She would sometimes come by to see us, but my mother never let us open the door. I mean we were like little prisoners. I remember my brothers being excited when they would hear the door and peek out the shades, seeing my aunt they knew she was going to have presents for us. However, when they went to moms' room door and told her that Sister was outside, she would hurriedly and quietly tell them they better not open her door, and to be quiet. The only time my mother was ever really happy to see my aunt was when she needed to borrow some money.

The only family members that we could talk to were our cousins who lived in the same projects. They were actually my mother's first cousins. They were in the cult also, and her male cousin was one of the elders in the cult. He had four kids all close in age to me and my siblings.

You know, serious change really never gives a warning. In fact most times it just happens. If you are really lucky, life changes will happen like psychologists say they should (birth, puberty, coming-of-age, school graduation, marriage, midlife, retirement, death). If something traumatic happens within any of the early stages, it can have a great impact on the next stages, and in my case, impact a good portion of my entire life.

I never saw change coming, because I was 4 years old when it happened. As I mentioned to you, we knew nothing more than Sunday-Kingdom Hall, Tuesday-Kingdom Hall, Wednesday-Bible study at Elder's house, Thursday-

Family bible study at our house, Monday and Friday's were individual bible study. I didn't mind going to the Kingdom Hall because even though we could not talk, and there was no singing there, for about 5-10 minutes after service was over, the kids had the opportunity to just be kids. We were able to run, and play almost like normal kids. However, it was Wednesday evenings that I grew to hate.

The Elders' house is where we had bible study on Wednesday evening. For us it was cool because the elder just happen to be my mother's first cousin Frank. We would spend an hour or so doing the bible stuff, and then afterward my mother would hang around and visit with Frank and his wife Betty. This would be the extent of my mother's weekly social outlet.

I enjoyed those first few times going there after we moved to Savannah. I would get to play with all the toys at their house that we did not have at mine. My brothers would get to play outside for a few moments, and my sister had other girls around her age to talk to.

One evening, right after bible study, my older cousin Jr. told my mom that he was going to take me into the kitchen to give me a snack, like he usually did. Jr. was always nice to me, and for a 17 year old he seemed to really pay attention to me.

This night was different though, because right after he gave me the snack, he told me to come outside with him, and I did. After we were outside where I could not see my siblings, and no one could see us, Jr. pulled me on the side of the house and pulled his penis out of his pants. He told me, "Touch it." I said "No." He whispered, "Don't be scared. Just touch it".

I was scared, because even though I had never seen the private parts of a boy before, I knew that it was something so dirty about it. With great hesitation and fear, I did touch his penis. I don't really know what I was feeling, but I knew that I was thinking that something was really wrong with this. He only made me rub it a little bit, but before he agreed to take me back in the house, he told me not to tell. "This is our secret." he murmured. I thought…No this was *my secret*, because I would have to carry it *all* by myself for years.

All that night after we got home, I was beside myself?! I knew that something very wrong happened, but I didn't know who to tell. I was scared of what my father would do to me if he found out, or what would happen to my family if I told my mother. This was the only family or friends that she had, so how could I be so selfish as to destroy that?

The next week the same things happen. This time because I was crying he took me to where I could see my mother from the window, as he played between my legs. I wanted someone to come find me, just to help me. Even at 4 years old, I found out what it felt like to feel dirty, as I wiped cum from my mouth.

Some Wednesdays when Jr. would go through his routine I would tell my mother that I did not want a snack. But she would tell me "Girl, go ahead with Jr.! All he wants to do is give you a snack." I wanted to scream, "No! All he wants to do is touch me, and make me suck on his penis!" But I was always too scared to say anything, because the child in me just felt like somehow I would still get in trouble for it.

My mother forced me, for the next three years to keep going to bible study, and to the place where my little mind would be forever changed and damaged. I think I was about 7 when my cousin Jr. was not able to molest me because we had moved from Hitch Village, so we had to attend bible study somewhere else.

At the time the sexual abuse began, the physical abuse from my parents got worse, so even home was not a refuge for me. For example, my father would routinely come home and if he found one thing wrong, or one person did anything that they had no business doing, we *all* had to pay for it! My father had a weightlifter's belt, which was thicker and heavier than any belt that they make today. This was his weapon of choice, and we were forced to lay across the bed with no clothes on to take our punishments. Any attempts to squirm away from the belt were pointless because it would only make my father's lashes longer and harder.

Needless to say, I never felt safe in my home, but there was one day that will stand in my mind forever as the day I lost all respect for my mother. It was a normal day. I was locked inside the house with my little sister, and my brothers were outside playing. My father came home, and I knew that things were not going to go well when he called them, and they did not come running. My mother was in her room sleeping, so she could go to work that night. After my brothers did not answer daddy, he sat on the couch for a little while, and soon after my brothers came in the house.

Immediately after they entered the house, my father announced that he was about to whip their asses. My brother Ronald went first and after all the beating, screams, and begging, he was free to go cry in his room. Well, then it was Donald's turn, and somehow something went very wrong. My father really lost it! He beat my brother so badly that he was on the floor saying that he could not walk. I was watching from the kitchen and scared to death. There my brother was dragging his body across the floor, and my father was over him beating and beating with that iron-mans belt. He kept hitting him and saying, "Get up! Get up!" But all Donald could do is scream for my mother. As he slid his body right up to my mother's door and begged her to save him, my father went in the closet and pulled out a policeman's night stick (a black jack). He then hit Donald with it, and I could hear my mother say "You better leave from my door!" My brother pleaded, "He is killing me!" My heart raced as I prepared for my mother's involvement in the situation, instead she uttered, "I *said*, leave from my door!" My father clinched his teeth as he reared back with the stick again and smacked Donald's leg.

Finally, after my brother seemed like the life was going to leave his 70 pound body, my mother open the door. She nonchalantly looked at my father and said, "That's enough Edlee". My chest still grips with terror from that day. I could not believe that her child nearly lost the use of his legs, and possibly his life in order for her to find the courage to help us. She didn't even scream at my *father* like she had when she insisted that Donald remove himself from her door.

Consequently, I would find that my father was not the only monster that we were living with during that time, because my mothers' weapon of choice was the brown extension cord. This was particularly brutal because blood could be, and was usually drawn when she dished out her punishments. Her beatings were usually given out for us doing anything that went against the Jehovah's Witness religion, or being disobedient to her. Unlike my father, I don't really think she took much pleasure in hitting us. Her beatings didn't seem to go on forever like my father's punishments. My father could start, stop, then start again, but mom just got things over with quickly.

Well, after getting used to the Hitch Village Projects for a while, my parents finally moved us into a house on the other side of town in 1980. It was a very quiet neighborhood, except for the days that my father would be cursing and yelling in the front yard, or passed out drunk in the back yard. This area had not been integrated fully. Our family was one of about a hand full of black families that they allowed to move in that area. But my mom said that we were moving here because it was a "safer place to live." Well, I remember they said that about Savannah before we moved down here and got all of our stuff stolen, so I didn't trust that statement anymore.

On a typical day on 69th street, I could actually play outside on the side or in front of the house. My brothers were older so they were allowed play on other streets or out of the neighborhood, as long as they were in the house by the time the streetlights came on. I had one friend named Karen who played with me, but she lived two streets away, so we were limited in our contact. My brothers would take me with them and drop me off at her house many days during the summer, so I would not have to follow them. My mother was working so much by then that we were not going to the Kingdom Hall much. That was great for me. My father was working more, but not drinking any less. At least he was not home terrorizing or screaming at the kids.

Well the day that would build the coffin for my childhood started out like most. I was ten years old. It was a Saturday and we woke up early to get our chores done so we could go outside and play later. Soon after Soul Train went off, my brothers left the house. I am not sure where Sherry was. By then she was 16, so most of her time was spent in her room waiting and wishing for the day that she was old enough to move out. I was outside alone making mud pies, and taking breaks to ride on the bike which my brother had put together for me from scrap parts.

I felt no sense of fear as the cars drove up and down the street, because I knew I was safe as long as I rode close enough to the curb. So as this one car gently eased up and down the street, I had no idea that this was the lion in the wilderness, and I was soon to be its prey.

As the car slowed the third time that it passed me, the white man that drove it called out to me, "Hey, have you seen a puppy?" I looked up from the mud ball that I was shaping, tried to focus on what he had just asked, and replied "No."

Well, all this time, my mother took great care to tell us all about Jehovah, and what was expected of us, but she never told us to be very aware of strangers. I never remember her saying that not all white people are good. All I ever remember her and the other adults in my life saying was the lighter a person's skin, the more they were to be trusted. I truly believed them. So as I sat on my bike, and rode down the street I saw the car coming back. I just figured that he had not found his puppy yet. It was not until the car stopped, and he jumped out and grabbed me off my bike that I knew something was definitely not right.

The gun that he had to my head made me paralyzed with fear. It happened so quickly that I don't remember screaming loud enough. The street was lonely, so I knew that no one saw him grab me. As soon as he had me in the car, he pulled my shirt over my head covering my face from being able to see him. Then he began to rub my chest. I didn't have much up there, because my breasts were still about 2 years away. I was crying and begging him to stop touching me. He told me not to scream or he would kill me. I quickly silenced my cries, and just let the tears flow without a word. It seemed that he drove me around forever. Finally, the car came to a stop.

When he pulled me out of the car, I could tell that we were in the woods. I had no idea where I was, or if I would ever see my family again. I was wondering if someone had noticed that I was missing, and if they would find me. As he placed the gun back to my head and forced me to grab my ankles and warned if I let go he would shoot me, I felt a pain that was worse than any beating that I had ever endured. I wept silently as the warm blood ran down my legs because I was too terrified to scream.

My first sexual experience came by the way of rape. I am not sure how long I was raped, or if it was just one time, because I either blacked out for a while, or God has blocked it from my memory. All I remember is him throwing me in the car and driving me to another secluded area. When the car stopped again, I remember crying and begging him not to hurt me again. Then I didn't even see his face, but I remember the harsh way he told me that if I told anyone that he would come back and kill my entire family. Then I remember him pushing me out of his car leaving me in the woods somewhere, bleeding and cast out like an unwanted dog

I don't remember how I got home, or when, because some things are just too painful. However, I do remember being at the hospital with all of these nurses, and police asking me questions. I remember them having to give me medication because they had to sew up my vagina and my rectum. I remember my mother being there, but not my father.

I came home, and the only person that would speak to me was Sherry. We were in our room, and she asked me if he made me suck his penis. I told her "No." She replied, "That's good that he didn't make you do that!" I understood what she was saying, because at that moment I remembered how Jr. would force me to suck him, and how nasty that taste would be for me. It seemed like it would take forever to get that nasty taste out of my mouth. So in that moment I actually appreciated my sister for making me look at the bright side of rape.

I am not sure if my brothers knew what happened. If they did, they chose to treat me the same way my father did; like I did not matter.

Well going back to school for me was very painful, because not only did I have the stitches in all of my private parts still reminding me of what had happen to me days earlier, I also was made very aware that everyone in my neighborhood, and at my school knew what had happen. See during those days the news papers were not like they are today. Reporters could not use your name in the paper if you were a minor, but they could say "A 10 year old girl living at 1302 E. 69th street was raped yesterday." Now if I were living in the house with 20 other 10 year old girls, then my identity would have been protected, but as luck would have it, there was only one. Then the people that did not read it in the paper (my teachers) had the *pleasure* of hearing it first hand from my mother. Then I had the displeasure of hearing my teacher, Mr. Slack talking about the rape to the other teachers that he gossiped with during recess. I also had to watch them smiling at me with pity, and pretend that I didn't just overhear them talking about me.

Well, if the rape was the coffin, let me illustrate to you the hammer and nail that sealed the coffin. After the rape I went into my own little world, where I didn't talk, didn't play, was scared to sleep, and didn't eat much either.

So, one day I heard my mother saying, "Edlee, I think we need to take Lisa to talk to a counselor."

I was standing in the door of my room when I heard my father say, "I am not paying for her to go and talk to no damn body. It's her fault that happened to her, because if she was inside the house and not on that bike, that would never have happened."

That statement wounded me for life right there! I was dealing with the rape the best that I could, and trying to just put it behind me, and do like my mother said when she told me, "Just don't talk about it to anyone." It became another one of those secrets that I was not allowed to tell, or ever mention.

To hear my father say that it was my fault that some pervert kidnapped, raped, and left me to die was more than my young mind could absorb. However, I felt it must be true, because my mom never told my daddy that he was an asshole for saying that. Ironically, she never took me to talk to the counselor.

In fact, I am sure you want to know if I ever got the courage to tell my mother what Jr. had done to me for all of those years. Yes, I did tell her when I was about 13 years old. Mom was not outraged, she didn't get on the phone and call her cousin to tell him that his son was and maybe still is a pedophile and molester. She didn't cry like I thought she would, and tell me how sorry she was that I had to go through this. No, she told me "Witnesses don't do those things!" I looked at her and said, "Well he did!" That is when she said, "Well, don't talk about it."

During that same conversation she told me how her stepfather fondled her when she was 9, but she did not want to hurt her mother, so she never told or talked about it. That was my hint as to why I could not say anything, because it would have hurt her friendship with her cousin. And so that too became one of those "elephants" that lived in my house, that no one could see but me.

Even after I became an adult, I would mention Jr. molesting me, and she would always act as if it was the first time she ever heard me tell her what he had done. However, I would receive the same response of her being angry with me for weeks or even months. Sometimes she would even turn my brothers against me. All in all, I have concluded that she does that to hide the pain and shame of not protecting me.

Moving on to what would be the next phase in my life was very hard considering all of these secrets that I carried like a badge of honor. These were the family secrets that stole my childhood, destroyed my peace, and killed the person that I could have been.

CHAPTER 3
My Soul Responsibility

To me, children are Gods way of showing you who you really are, and who you're not. My aunt Barbara, the Prophetess in the family, would say they are gifts from God. Now I would rebut that by saying that for every gift I have ever received there were folded up papers along with them called INSTRUCTIONS.

I mean just think about it for a moment, if you buy a bottle of *perfume* on the back of the box it will tell you what it is made from and usually how to use it. Now even kids at the ripe old age of 1-year old know what "smell good stuff" is and how to use it, so why would we need instructions? I will tell you! It's because the makers of this item don't want to run the risk of you going wrong. They don't need people suing them because they sprayed it in their mouth, and are now heaving-sick. Oh, and the instructions will tell you where not to spray the perfume; like don't spray on your genitals, because you may get a burning that you would not soon forget. However, you will only make that mistake once. This is why instructions are so important. So on simple things we get instructions, but God sends us complex little souls that we are responsible for without the benefit of instructions.

I have had children at every stage in my life, and each of them have come with their own personality, hang ups, demands, issues, looks, and more importantly, they arrived in my life under very different circumstances. However, none of them came giving me manna from heaven, or instructions on how to cause the least amount of harm to them. Those are just things I had to learn along the way. However, I was forced to parent my children with some of the skills that I learned from my own parents. So let me show you how my parenting has evolved throughout my lifetime.

It was June 3, 1984 when I conceived Daniel. I remember that day so well, because up until that day sex had always been forced on me by people I felt powerless to say "no" to. It had been two or three years since the rape, and I was trying to be normal. Ed and I had met in middle school, when I was really going through my "Who am I?" stage. I felt ugly most days, and my self-esteem was below the floor, but the first day I laid eyes on Edwin, he smiled at me with perfect straight white teeth. Before that day no one had ever really smiled at me. I mean, most of the smiles were ones of pity. Therefore, when he smiled at me and said, "Hey, what's your name?" I felt like a shiny new penny. I replied, "Mona, but some people call me Lisa." Then he said, "Well, I will call you Lisa." From that moment we became like twins. For many months we did everything together. Being so young gave us the beauty of dating the way it should be done. We didn't think about sex. We enjoyed spending time together. Our best times were going walking, running in the rain, climbing trees, playing pinball, and riding bikes. He would take me all the way across town on the handlebar of his bike, and I would not be scared at all of falling off and breaking my front teeth.

It took Ed about four weeks before he asked me if I would let him kiss me. Though neither of use had every really kissed anyone else, we used the entire spring to practice.

June 3 was the last day of school, and as we walked home wondering how we would see each other during the long summer, he said to me that if I really loved him I would "do it" with him. Yep, he said "do it"! I didn't want to lose the only person that was nice to me, and that always made time for me, so I secretly went off with him and met his request. For the next 6 weeks we would *have sex* everyday. It didn't mean anything to me, and if the truth be told, I didn't enjoy it because every time he laid on me I tried to blank out until it was over. I was still trying to get over all of the unhealthy, forced sex that I had encountered. It was very hard for me not to view him the same way I did all the other males.

I didn't even notice that I had missed my cycle, until my mom asked me one day. I guess I was looking differently, but I could not tell. When I told her that I didn't remember having a cycle for two months, she took me to the doctor. Well, there went my life as I knew it. I was pregnant.

It seemed as if I would never stop being pregnant with Daniel. That was the longest 9 months of my life! I had no idea what to expect because this was my first pregnancy, so my body was doing things that I was not sure should be happening; like going from not showing at all, to looking like I was hiding a baby seal under my coat. Oh, and my favorite was going to the bathroom four times an hour, and being mad as hell for no apparent reason at all.

I fought more when I was pregnant with Daniel than any other time in my life. Just saying "hello" to me during that time could win you a butt-whipping that you would not soon forget. I actually remember a girl bullying my friend Noel (she would later become my sister-in-law). Noel told me about Nikki beating her up on the train tracks, and I vowed in my heart that I was gonna get that *heifer*. So that morning, my four months pregnant self put an extension cord in my pocket, because I was pissed. I waited outside the school gate, and as soon as Nikki got out there, I went up to her and said, "Bully me!" I am sure I was cursing like a sailor, because I could put adjectives together during that time just like my daddy. So as she was trying to get her courage up, I took the opportunity to slap her in the face. *Then* I commenced to stomping her on the ground, and *then* I pulled out my cord and whipped her. At some point, I didn't even notice that she had sat on the ground, and given up. I also did not notice Ed coming to where we were until I felt him pick me up and toss me to the other side of the street. All the time he was saying "You know your pregnant, what you trying to do lose the baby?!" The cat was out the bag, because up until then no one knew that I was pregnant.

Those are the things that I could not expect to happen to my personality and my body. However, things also happened during that time that I would not have imagined or expected. Well, the moment my mother brought me home after finding out that I was pregnant, *I sneaked two calls out of the prison.* The first call that I made was to my best friend Angie, then the next was to Ed (I had to warn him that hurricane Marie was on the path headed straight to him). How was I to know that within one week I would lose my best friend, and my boyfriend? Angie's mother told her that she could not hang out with me anymore? Then Ed's grandfather put him on punishment and forbade him from seeing or speaking to me.

Ed had been living with his grandparents, the Reid's, since he was about two years old. Mr. Reid was Ed's grandfather, and he was the darkest, tallest, loudest, scariest and most definitely the ugliest man I had ever met in my life, up to that point. He was about 6'2", and was greasy black like tar. He had big pink lips, and one side of his face looked like he had been mauled by a wild animal or burned in a fire. Regardless of what happened, his personality was uglier than his face.

Mr. Reid controlled everything in his life, and in the lives of his family. Since he had been taking care of Ed since he was 5, he controlled him also. Mr. Reid was a longshoreman at the ports of Savannah. He had what they call "long money", but was very tight with it.

When my mom told him that I was pregnant, and she was making me keep the baby, he was pissed. Mr. Reid had an opinion about girls like me who got pregnant. He told me that I would never be anything. He said that I was trying to trick his son because his father had money. He told my mom that he would never live long enough to spend all of the money he had saved over the years, and that we were just common trash.

My mom had an opinion about him also, and it was not a good one at all. She often times during those nine months talked about him to her friend, and to his face. Mom would not say much to my father when he acted the fool, but she stood up to that black bully, Mr. Reid, like she was 6'2". Even though she knew it was not right that I was a little girl having a baby, she never put all of the blame on me like others did. She gave Ed equal flack in the situation, and that made me feel a little better. However, I knew that mom was embarrassed by my pregnancy, because she made it her business not to take me to any doctor were she could possibly see any of her Jehovah's Witnesses friends. She worked at Candler Hospital in the nursery and she had health insurance for me, so I could have had Daniel right there, but she made it her business to send me to Memorial Hospital so that no one at her job would have to know "her business", and she got me a private room so that no one would see her visiting me.

Ed did not speak to me out of fear of his grandfather from the time I was 4 months pregnant, until I was 9 months. That was so hard for me. I think that everyday I cried, and when I was not crying I was just down right hating life. The only thing that I had was school, and I was not doing to well in it. I was grouped with other girls who were pregnant like me, and our principal Mr. Speed even asked my mother to allow me to quit school because he could not assure my safety, and he felt like I was setting a bad example for other young girls.

I know that you are wondering how my father felt about this "gift" from God that I was carrying. Well, let's just say that the same bitches and whores that he called me from the time that *I got myself raped*, I was still all of them and about 1000 more. Not one day went by that he was not hurling insults at me. However, by that time I had started fighting… even him!

I remember December 27, 1984 well because just three days prior to that my mother received the call from New York that her brother George had been robbed and murdered. After they brought the body back to Savannah, mom had been spending time in Garden City with her family. I spent all of my time at home, because even though I am sure mom told Barbara that I was pregnant, she did not want anyone to see me.

That day I was sitting in our living room playing in Nikki's hair. Daddy was home and had been drinking as usual. My brothers went to the funeral with mom, and Sherry had finally moved out of the house, and was married. During this time my father spent much of his time telling me how worthless I was, but my mother made sure he did not hit me. But that day I did not have her to protect me. I don't remember exactly what I said to him, but I do remember him telling me to do something, and I did not comply. The next thing I remember is him coming and slapping me in the face. I mean things went dark for a second, he slapped me so hard.

I sat there for a second, because my sister was sitting right in front of me, but in the corner of my eye I could see a two by four board sitting on the floor because we were having work done in the house. As I looked at the board, I slid silently over there, like a ninja. Daddy had gone into the dining room, acting like he had the victory. What he didn't know is that was the day I vowed he was never going to beat, or hit me again.

Out of nowhere I came behind him and waged my attack. I beat him with everything in me. I hit him for the years of pain that he had caused me and my brothers. I hit him for causing my sister Sherry to run away from home, leaving me alone with them. I hit him for the times that I saw him choke my mother, and spit in her face. I hit him for not being a provider. I hit him for not being a man. Then I ran out of the house to my neighbors and told them what I had done.

My neighbors didn't call the police, but somehow they got in touch with my mother. When they put me on the phone with her, she said in a muffled voice, so that her sisters could not hear her, "What is going on there?" All I said was, "I am going to kill your husband, and you will be at another funeral by next week". Mom was mad as she coarsely replied "I will talk to ya'll when I get home." I said "Fine" and hung up the phone.

When she got home that night, I cursed as I was telling her that I was not going to let that man hit me anymore. She was enraged by my disrespect, but she realized that all of those years of his abuse had grown a monster in me also, and I was fighting back.

It was just me and my mother at the hospital the day I went into labor. Mom had sworn Mr. Reid as her arch enemy, but she did call him when I went into labor. Obviously he didn't care much because he didn't show up, and he put Ed on punishment and warned him what would happen if he even thought that he had gone within blocks of the hospital we were in. As a side note, the hospital was exactly 19 walking blocks, and 5 driving minutes from his house. But he was a no show also. My father could care less if I was having a baby or open heart surgery that day, but he didn't come near the hospital *either*. None of my brothers, or sisters came *either*. I felt like I had been disfellowshipped out of my own family!

The day that I went into labor I thought I was home free. I thought that everything would go smoothly because my whole pregnancy had been horrible, so things couldn't possibly get worse. Uh, yes they can!

I had been in labor for 24 hours without the luxury of an epidural when I heard the doctor tell my mother that I was not doing well, and the baby was going to die unless surgery was preformed right away. Somehow active Daniel had managed to get tied up in his cord. So they had to cut me to get him out.

When I woke up from surgery my life had changed forever. Daniel Jerome is what I named him. "Daniel" after the Cabbage Patch doll my mom had brought me years earlier and "Jerome" after his father. I could not name him Edwin, because first that was an old name that had been used too much in history, and two because I didn't want my father to think that I would *ever, ever, ever* name any of my children after him.

Days after bringing Daniel home something started happening with me that I could not explain. I would sit in my room looking at him and crying for many days. I mean if he cried, I cried. I would look at him and just think how he was my responsibility. I had to be everything to this little person, and at that point I didn't even know enough about my own self to take care of me. In addition to the crying, I also had flashes. Flashes to me are like visions. They only last for a second or two, but the pictures that are imprinted in your mind are like mini movies. It seemed that I was having lots of flashes of me doing bad things to Daniel. I loved my child, but my mind was making me believe that I didn't. I didn't know until many years later that this was postpartum depression, and psychosis. I didn't know because I was too scared to tell anyone that I had thoughts of killing my baby. My mother called it "The Baby Blues" but that only minimized how I was truly feeling.

By the time Daniel was 3 months old, I got tired of being the only one responsible for looking after him. I was overwhelmed with being a mother, and the depression was getting the best of me. So in a stunt that every single mother has thought of a time or two and even done, I packed Daniel up one summer day, put him in his carrier, and took him to Ed's house. Ed was still scared to talk to me, even though his grandfather was providing clothes, diapers, and milk for Daniel. He had not seen Daniel yet. So when I showed up on his back porch, he would not let me in. He opened the door and quickly closed it back. So I just left, but I left without Daniel. I said to myself, this Negro is going to get this boy *today!* So when I called him from the phone booth down the street and told him that his child was on the porch, he had no other choice but to get him and take him in the house. By the time I came back, Ed and his cousin Roddrick had taken Daniel in the house, and Ed was trying to take care of Daniel. That day, when Mr. Reid came home, Ed stood up to him and said that he wanted Daniel to be there with him. Mr. Reid realized that Ed was growing up, and controlling him was getting harder. Therefore he began to let us come over on a regular basis.

By the time Daniel was about 10 months old, my depression got worse, and my behavior was more than my mother could take. So one day she put me in the car, and took me for what would be my *intervention*. I was locked up in Charter, which is a mental hospital, for 3 months. Strangely just as my insurance was about to stop paying for my incarceration, I was cured!

By March of that year I was out of the hospital, and dating Edwin again. It made me feel good to see how much Ed cared for Daniel, even while I was away. It seemed that for the next year things were pretty good with us. Everywhere that Ed went he would pack me and Daniel up and take us. He had his first real job at 16 and he made sure Daniel had the Nike shoes, and all the nicest clothes. I was still living with my parents, and nothing much had changed there, but things were relatively okay. I just had to sit through a lecture from my mother once or twice a week.

Ed and I dropped out of school almost 18 months after Daniel was born. Ed really wanted to do something with his life at that time, so he joined the Job Corp in the summer of 1986. I didn't know what I wanted to do so I started working on obtaining my GED. We wrote each other everyday, and talked daily also, so the time apart was not so bad. By the time he came home in December for a visit, I was more than ready to see him. It was a great Christmas, and New Year for me and Daniel. We spent it at Ed's house, and Daniel got all kinds of toys and clothes from Ed and his grandfather. When Ed went back to Job Corp, I was glad because he had come home right after my cycle went off, and he left two days before it was scheduled to come back. Perfect timing, so I thought.

Well, on Jan. 5, 1987 I was expecting my cycle to start, but it did not. I started to get very nervous. I pulled out the calendar praying that I was confused about the first day of my last period. Lady luck was not on my side, but "Danielle" was definitely inside.

I didn't tell anyone besides Ed that I was pregnant until I was about 5 months. I found comfort in talking to Daniel about my problems, but he was 2 years old and not talking much so I knew he would keep this secret about the baby. Ed and I said that if it didn't just go away, we were going to save up money for an abortion. I wanted it to go away, because I didn't know what an abortion really was at that time, but I sort of felt it was not for me. I took some pills that were supposed to cause my period to come, but they did not work. I was desperate not to have to face my mother with another baby.

However, after many months of hiding, I finally had to tell her that I was pregnant. The day started with me putting on Daniel's clothes and mine. I would always make sure that I was covered up before leaving out of the room so my secret would not be revealed. This day was different because I had not been feeling well for days, but now I could not stop throwing up. These violent projections of the content of my stomach lead to sharp pains in my stomach by that afternoon. So I went to my mother's room where she always locked herself away when she was not working.

She took one look at me and asked me what was wrong. My eyes always gave me away whether I was sick, upset, happy, or sad. So it was in that moment that I told her I was sick and my stomach was hurting. She questioned me about what I ate, and I told her that I had not really eaten in days. Then she asked me if I was pregnant. I looked away as I told her that I thought I was pregnant. She shouted as she asked "When was your last period?" I lied and said "I think it was in February." She told me to get dressed and took me to the emergency room.

As we sat answering questions with the nurse, I knew that it would not take the doctors long to find out that I was very far along. I could feel the kicking and moving already. So when the nurse announced that the doctor wanted to have an ultrasound done on me. I looked at my mother knowing that it would not be long before her pissed-off look became actual anger.

The ultrasound took less than a half hour to complete, and then they rolled me in a wheelchair back to my room. About fifteen minutes later the doctor came back to my room. He announced to me and my mother that I was dehydrated. Then he paused a moment before he told my mother that I was twenty two weeks pregnant. My mother responded by asking if the baby was okay. The doctor said that from what the test results stated, the baby was fine.

It did not go away, and on September 8, 1987 there was my little girl. In my heart I wanted another little boy, but the day I laid eyes on Danielle I fell in love. She was perfect. She had "good hair" that I could fix. She was not too fat or too small. She was the perfect 6 lbs 14 oz. Ed was right there at the hospital the night she was born, and right after she got here he ran home to get his wallet with his license in it, because he wanted her to have his last name. This was big to him because Daniel was a Stewart, and he did not want anymore of his children carrying my father's last name. I named her Danielle Shantell Rosa; "Danielle" after the other Cabbage Patch doll that I had, "Shantell" because I just liked that name; and "Rosa" after my great grandmother.

Mom kicked me out of the house by the time I was 16. I bounced from pillow to post for a while. Danielle was about 6 months old when my mother put me in my own apartment. I was forced to become an adult for real! In addition to being out on my own, Ed had begun to change also. He had a cousin named Roderick that lived with him that had introduced him to drugs. He started with weed, but by the time he was 18 he was cracked out, and I was a real single mother. All of my hopes that we would one day get married and raise our kids together were gone. In addition to that, soon after Danielle was born postpartum depression set in again.

By the time a year had gone by, I was in the pits of hell, just wanting a mist of cool water. My life sucked. I had lost my friend, babies' father, and boyfriend to drugs. The only men that were coming around were the ones that knew I had my own apartment, and they could come and lay up for free. I would allow them because by that time I had no self worth. What little self esteem I did have left was given away because of my need to feed my kids on a daily basis. Therefore, having sex with men that pretended to care for me, so that I could buy food for my children is how the first six months of my adult living went.

I am sure that is why I didn't even know when I became pregnant in 1988. I didn't know who the father was either. I know that it is sad, and some may even say trifling, but I had no idea who aside from me was responsible for this baby that I was expecting. The only thing that I did know was that I had two kids already. I was living in an apartment with no stove or refrigerator. My rent was $210 a month, and I was getting $235 in welfare, and $189 in food stamps. We were cold and hungry most of the times, and I had no one that I could call. My mother felt that her job was done the day she moved me into that apartment. My sister Sherry, whom I always depend on, was dealing with marital issues of her own, so I limited my calls to her. My brothers had never taken an interest in my needs, so talking to any of them would have been pointless. I knew having another baby was absolutely not what I needed.

Having an abortion this time was not an option. I was broke, and I barely had money to keep the lights on. That was why had to sell my food stamps every month. Therefore I knew coming up with the $320 for an abortion was impossible. I suspected the baby was Ed's but by this time he was busy stealing Danielle's diaper and formula money to buy drugs, and figuring out a way to pawn the only TV and VCR I had.

So I knew asking him for money for an abortion was out of the question. I was having little interludes with Corey (my friend since middle school) when he appeared every now and then, because he would give me money. Then for about two months after I moved in a man named Greg from Florida lived with me and we had sex once. So there you have it, three people could have been "the one." I would have needed the Maury show to find my "baby-daddy".

I suddenly made up my mind, for once in my life to start making decisions for myself. Up to that point *life* had just happened to me. So I looked in the phone book, and saw an ad that read "Are you Pregnant? Scared? Need Help?" My answer was affirmative to all three questions, and that lead me to calling The Parent and Child Development Center. The person on the phone took my information and set an appointment for the next day.

I walked into the office pretty scared because this was my first time ever taking care of any business matters on my own. However, the atmosphere of the office was very relaxed, and the very tall, slim, white woman that greeted me in the lobby calmed my fast-beating heart when she introduced herself. She told me I could call her by her first name, Jessica.

She seemed very concerned for me and my child. She asked me questions like who the father was, and where were my own parents and family. I told her the whole sad story about how I had two kids that I was struggling with, a baby daddy that was strung out on drugs, and parents that wanted me and my kids anywhere but in their home. Oh, and a host of uncles, aunts, and cousins that hardly even knew me, thanks to the Jehovah's Witnesses. So she began grooming me for a major decision that I would have less than 4 months to make.

I looked at my two little ones during that time and I would become sad because all I could see is the effects of poverty in their lives. Danielle was not guided by nature, or age as to when she became potty trained. She was guided by the fact that I had no money to buy pull-ups or pampers. Many days she had to wear shorts to bed and because she hated being wet, she potty trained before she was 18 months old. Daniel's hair was not cut on a regular basis like it should have been, so he had a mini-afro, which was not at all cool during that time. I had a hot plate that I cooked every meal on, and most of those meals were grits and eggs, since when I was able to get a refrigerator, it was the kind you would have in a dorm room. So buying more than one pack of meat or a gallon of milk was out of the question. And I had one pot and one small pan, so there was no way possible for me to make a gourmet meal. Then we had mice that made it hard for me to sleep around there, because I was always hoping that they would not get in the bed with the kids, or eat the bread before we could. I would routinely not eat meals, because I was trying to save food for the kids. So all I knew when I was thinking of making the biggest decision of my life is that I didn't want any other kids to have to suffer like Daniel and Danielle were. As a result of this reality, I decided to give my baby up for adoption.

Yes, you heard me. I decided to give my baby up for adoption. I am very much black, and suddenly I was making such a "white" decision. Not that I am a racist or anything, but if you ask one hundred black people if they know someone who has put their child up for adoption, 95 will say "No!" The others will ask you if it counts when DFCS comes and takes them from you for neglect, because that is usually the only way that a black person is going to give up their child. Most of us forget about the fact that we can't take care of that child, or the fact that there is a family out there that has the means and desire to provide a good home for the "accident" that was made; on the other hand, most black families will bring them home anyway, and hope for the best. Well not me! Not that time! I felt that it would have been totally selfish of me to bring that baby home, knowing what home was like. I feel that we would have far less suffering in this world if people knew their limits, and were willing to make the tough decisions when life gave them something totally unexpected.

Well, I had my daughter on June 26, 1989, and yes I went through with it. I didn't want to see her when she was born, and there was no one there at the hospital when I delivered but my mother. I felt she was only there because she was hoping to talk me out of putting her up for adoption. After I delivered, they rushed her out of the room, because I gave strict instructions that I did not want anyone to see her. But something in me could not just forget about her, like she never existed. So on the second day I told them that I wanted to see her.

When the nurse came in with her I could see she had a head full of hair. As they placed her in my arms, I searched her face looking to see who she looked like. Just then there was a visitor from the next bed in there with a camera. He asked me if I wanted him to take a picture of me and my baby with his automatic Polaroid, I said "No." He pleaded, "Come on, you may want to remember this some day." I consented after looking down at her soft, pretty face. At that moment I realized that even though I had two kinds prior to this one, no one had ever cared enough to record the days of their births. But this one was special because she took a picture with me.

The day that I left the hospital I had a few final things to do. First, I had to sign more papers, which gave me a funny feeling the entire time. The next thing they sprung on me was that I had to name the baby. Wow, I had never thought of her as mine, so I didn't come up with any good names. So, I looked at her, and I called her Vandy. Vandy was actually the name of a friend of mine back then. But he was so funny and so nice that I felt it would be a perfect name for her. Then I packed my things and had them call me a cab, and I left my precious Vandy behind.

Danielle and Daniel were as different as night and day. Daniel was always more outgoing and adventurous than Danielle. Danielle was always quiet, and easy to cry.

Daniel was a bully, but also a protector of Danielle. Even though Danielle did not talk much, she was always smart, enlightened, and she protected Daniel also. What I really remember about them together is their closeness. I mean there was no closer pair than those two. It sometimes felt like them against me in our home. They were always finding ways to outwit me, and I was always trying to stay one step ahead of whatever they were going to get into next. From flooding their bedroom by turning a chest into a bathtub, to jumping off the top of the house and almost breaking both legs and an arm, to keeping secrets that to this day they keep for each other, to fighting in the street, they did it all together. I found that my parenting was much like my parents, except it took a lot more to make me result in spanking, and only the guilty party had to receive the punishment.

Well, I said after Vandy was born that I never wanted to have anymore kids, yet I did not take the necessary steps to prevent that from happening. Corey and I had been together for a little more than a year, and he was a childhood friend, and my standby boyfriend for much of my life. I can admit that I didn't love him, but he was comfortable to me, so I stayed.

Needless to say, when I got pregnant in 1992, we were at a standoff. He didn't want us to go through the process of having an abortion, because just 5 months prior I had been pregnant, and on the very day that we drove down to Jacksonville to have the abortion, I had miscarried. I still didn't want another child. But he told me that I had to have her. I was happy that he was in my life, but I was mad most of the time because I just didn't want to be pregnant. There was nothing that he could do to make me happy. Then, me feeling like he was cheating didn't make things any better.

I didn't know it yet, but this pregnancy and birth would signal a major turning point in my life. Aside from my relationship with Corey', my home life was far from perfect. I was living in a rat infested apartment again on the west side of town. My next door neighbor was Nigerian from Nigeria. He spent most of his day getting on my nerves with the loud chanting that he would be doing in his apartment. Corey would come over in the evening and stay with me until late at night, and sometimes the kids and I would go and stay at his house.

I was only 23 and post-partum depression had set in once again. I needed something to live for, and being a mother just was not going to do it for me. When I looked at my kids, and thought of Vandy who was out there somewhere I realized that my life was a mess. I had very limited education, and had been through hell in the years leading up to this current birth. So life was not worth living for me.

Ukpong, who was my next door neighbor, was an African with a very strong voice. He was very nice to me and the kids. He would feed us at least twice a week. I don't think that he ever knew that those meals he gave me were some of the only meals that I had. Everyday I would hear him through the paper thin walls of our apartment for hours chanting. I did not know what he was saying, and I was so narrow minded during that time that I felt he was doing some roots or voodoo. So one day, being nosy changed my life.

It was a regular day. I went over to Ukpong's house to eat some African soup, and fufu which was off the chain good! While I was eating I got up the nerve to ask, "Hey Ukpong, are you over there putting a curse on my apartment?"

He laughed, "Why would you ask me that?"

I hesitated, "Because I hear you chanting everyday!"

I was also thinking about the many documentaries I had seen on the Discovery Channel about Voodoo doctors, witches, and people that were into the new religion, Wiccan.

He then smiled, looked warmly into my face and replied, "Do you know Jesus?"

I looked at him blankly, "No. Who is that?" Up to this point I had never heard the name "Jesus". The thought made me laugh to myself. My neighbor, Owoidogho Ukpong, "Ukpong" for short, had a name I could neither spell nor pronounce and I was thinking that this "Jesus" must be a friend or relative of his.

Then Ukpong picked up this thick, intimidating, black book, and announced, "John 1:1 says that God so loved the world that he gave his only son..."

I looked at him as if he had two heads and said, "Oh really?"

Then he said, "Jesus is a healer, deliverer, and risen savior."

I was intrigued by his deep words.

Ukpong went on talking and I stopped eating my only meal of the day. It was almost like the words that he spoke began to satisfy my hunger. Then he began to tell me about Heaven and where I would go if I died that day. He asked me, "Do you know that you're going to Heaven?"

I admitted that I didn't believe in Heaven or Hell. "When I die I go to the grave." I responded. That was the only answer I was sure of because my mother taught me that those places did not exist, and our bodies went back to dust after we die, and our souls are gone until the resurrection day when Jehovah decides who is worthy to come back and live on Earth.

Ukpong said calmly, "Mona, you can become new, all your sins can be forgiven, and you can live in Heaven after you leave this earth if you accept Jesus as your lord and savior."

I thought on his words because I had never had anything that I considered a lord, and surely my life did not reflect anyone that believed in a savior. Something was pulling on my heart to just say "Yes," so I looked at him and said, "I want to know Jesus."

Ukpong looked in the book that he had been reading to me from, and seemed to study for a moment. Then he said, "All you have to do is believe with your heart, and confess with your mouth that Jesus is Lord. You must believe that Jesus died for your sins, and that on the third day He got up with all power in His hands."

I started my confession of faith and salvation saying, "Lord, forgive all my sins…" I believed and repeated Ukpong as he spoke with his deep African accent. After I did all of this, I began to say "Thank you." I could not stop saying "Thank you." It was a grateful "Thank you", coming up from a deep place in me. My "Thank you" continued until it turned into an overwhelming "Thank you."

I didn't even realize that Ukpong had begun his chanting, until suddenly something happened. My tongue began to move on its own. I was no longer in control. My "Thank you" became a language that I had never spoken, heard, nor could I understand what I was saying. My mind wanted to regain control, but another part of me was saying "Just let go."

So I let go and went into another place. I fell to the floor and cried. It was as if I was pouring out all my hurt and pain. I was throwing up the places that my life had taken me, and this new found "Jesus" was changing some things in me. When I left Ukpong's house, my heart felt lighter.

I continued my new found prayer life going to Ukpong's house everyday to hear him talk about the Bible. He would also take the time to pray for me.

But I still had many trials to go through that would test my new faith. Oh, and it was about to happen. I only told Corey what happened at Ukpong's house.

I delivered Courtney on Aug 13, 1993. Corey was not at the hospital when I had her, but he made it there by noon. He was not really happy because just eight days before she was born his mother died, and I watched the man that I love die too. He tried to smile, and put on a good front for me, but I was sure that all he wanted to do was get in bed and wait for his daylight to come again. I had been there, in the depths of grief and depression, many times, so I knew what that felt like.

I was not very happy either, even though Ukpong had told me a little about Jesus, and now I could pray in tongues, I still did not have a true sense of just who God was in my life. I was even scared to pray outside of Ukpong's apartment because I thought that the only time I could turn on my tongues to God was at his place. After Courtney was born, I brought her home to this tiny two bedroom apartment. It was covered with old wood paneling, so it was dark. There were holes in the wall that lead to the outside, and wood rats would find their way in often. I also only had one air conditioner, so the kids and I slept in the same room for their safety and comfort.

I had no job, and welfare just was not enough money to take care of us. Many times I had to sell my food stamps just to pay a bill. It seemed like every week the kids would come home from school and we either did not have water, electricity, or an eviction notice was on the door. Finally, after months of trying to stay a step ahead of the bills, we were evicted and forced to live with Corey.

Things were pretty good for about two months after we moved in with Corey. I think God gives women the ability to know when something is not right, and if we would obey all of the signs we would be able to get out of situations much quicker. However, the other thing that God gives us is compassion and understanding, which is why we can see the trouble coming, but we will justify other people's actions with excuses that make no sense at all.

After weeks of him coming home later and later, and us not being as close as we were, I began to wonder where he was spending his time. I got my answer in November of 1993 when the doorbell rang. I went to the door and a very familiar face was standing there. It was Corey's baby mama. I knew there was gonna be some drama when I heard her say her name. So I opened the door with my baby in my hand, wanting her to see that we were a happy family. But she trumped me with what she was holding, not in her hand, but in front of her. Yep, she was pregnant! And the baby belonged to Corey! I was hurt, scared, and on the verge of homicide all in one minute.

I sat waiting on him to bring his black butt home. He finally came home, and I was sitting in the living room with the gun. I jumped on him as soon as he closed the door, and really considered killing him, but I thought about my freedom.

I was pissed because I didn't want another child, and he made me have Courtney, and now here he was cheating on me and about to have another child. I was also more aware of HIV at that time, so I was scared of what he may have brought to me.

After days of arguing Corey asked me to take my kids and leave his house. After crying and begging him to let me stay, I finally left. I left not knowing where I was going, or who I could go to. I walked around the corner to my grand aunt, Sister's, house. I knew that she was home, because the only time that she ever really left her home is when I would take her to the store. I saw her peek out the window, and I stood there with my baby in my arms waiting for the door to open. The door never came open, so I walked on. It seemed as if the pain of that day would never end, because I knew the kids would be home from school soon, but we had no place to go. I had no place to take them, but I knew that I did not want them outside with me. So, here I was staring down another hard decision that I had to make.

The kids got home about 3:30 and as we walked down the street I told them how much I loved them, and that I did not want them to be cold that night. They looked at me as if they really did not understand, and that is when I told them that we could not go back to Mr. Corey's house.

Daniel asked "So where are we going?", and I told him that I was taking him and Danielle to a place where they would be safe. I told him that I would not be able to stay, but other people would take good care of them, and I would return for them as soon as I could. Within hours, we were all standing on the front steps to Greenbrier Children Home, which was for kids that the State had taken or homeless kids. I knew that if I surrendered them to the Home that I had a good chance of getting them back, but if you were ever unlucky enough in Savannah to have your kids taken, you would catch hell trying to get them back.

That afternoon I signed my kids over, and walked away with Courtney in my hand, not knowing where we would rest for the night. I walked to a nearby park, and as night fell I tucked Courtney under my jacket, praying that I would keep enough heat to make her warm, and I laid my head on the picnic table and rested a little, and thought of what my next move had to be.

Daybreak came and I had to be on the move again. For days I would walk the streets of Savannah, in the same clothes that I left Corey's house in. I called him several times begging him to come and get his child, but when men harden their hearts towards you, there is nothing you can ever do or say to mend ways. I also realized that not only was he cheating on me with his children s' mother, but he had met another woman named Bea. I had only been gone for six days before he moved her and two of her children in his home. I was crushed as I saw her driving past me and my baby in the car that I used to drive. Approximately a week later, after sleeping outside, and going to public bathrooms to try to remove some of the dirt that I had accumulated on my body, I called Corey, and he had changed his number.

I now know that numbers have meanings, but I did not know that when all of this was happening in my life. Therefore, on the 8th day of this homeless journey I went to find a quiet park for Courtney and I to sleep. The weather had once more changed, and though it had been pretty cold the past few nights, it was freezing, and I did not know if we were going to make it through the night. I have never felt that sort of bitter cold before, but sometime during the night my body got numb, I didn't even realize when the police car pulled up.

I forced my eyes to focus, and my body not to panic and run, because I was so scared of the things that moved in the night. The previous night I had to run with my baby into a back alley to get away from a man that I knew was trying to use me as sexual prey. He didn't care that I was sitting on a bench crying with a baby in my arms. Therefore, when I saw the tall black man walking toward me alarms rang in my head.

He turned on his flashlight and looked at me and asked "Why are you in a park with that baby at 2 in the morning?" I told him, "I have no place to live. He asked me, "Are you a victim of domestic violence?" Hell that was like asking George Bush if he was Republican.

All I had ever known is abuse from every man that I had ever allowed into my world. If they were not physically abusing me, they could always fall back on the verbal, sexual, and mental abuse. So, "Yes" was my answer. He told me that he was going to take me to a safe place, where the baby and I could stay all day and not have to leave like most homeless shelters in this area.

He placed me and Courtney in the backseat with her dirty baby bag. I was grateful for the warmth of the police car. I could not even remember the last time I ate a meal, but feeding Courtney was all I ever worried about.

Walking into the Safe Shelter was oblivious to me. I remember the policeman telling me that everything would be okay, and then I remember a woman in her late 100's acting as if giving me a place to stay was the last thing on her mind. It was very late at night, and we had awaken her to do a job that I could tell she was not happy doing. She told me all the rules, and took me to a room that had bunk beds in it. I was finally able to get a shower, and breastfeed Courtney. It seems all at one time the reality of my situation had finally set in on me. My life was dark, too dark for daylight to ever come again.

Having grown up in the Jehovah's Witness religion, I always remember my mother telling us that when we die, or when Armageddon comes that we will live in peace, and the troubles of this world will not be with us anymore. Well, because I never went towards any religion when I got older, it was safe to say that I knew nothing about Gods will for my life, and that he wanted me to have peace, joy, and love in my current life. So with the Jehovah's Witness beliefs in mind I felt it was time for me to just die, and maybe I would have better luck in the next life. Of course, that was only if Jehovah found me worthy to bring back.

As I sat on the floor of the dark room looking into the face of a baby that knew nothing but my feelings, I could hear a voice telling me that if I were going to commit suicide that night I would have to take her also because she could not live without me. My mind was fixed on the fact that I had no hope for tomorrow. I had left my other children days before, not knowing what could have been happening to them, and now, here I was homeless, ashamed, and alone in a dark room not feeling loved, with no family support, and my only friend just abandoned me and had changed his number and was expecting another baby by the summer.

Even through the desperation and depression, I felt something else. I felt a need to talk, but there was no one with me. So I began to talk into the atmosphere. I had never really been taught to pray, and my brief brush with God up to this point had only been in Ukpong's house, and I was surely far from his house now. I wanted to ask God to forgive me for killing my child and myself, but something very strange happened after I began to talk.

My prayer was, "I don't know who you are, or if you are even real, but I know that unless you help me; my child and I are going to die tonight."

Well, that is not one of those long drawn out prayers that all of the deacons know how to send up to God, I didn't even say Amen, but it was the best I knew how to give. Up until that time I had never remembered really praying for myself at all, unless you count before meals, when my mom would make us say our uniform prayer to Jehovah.

I didn't know really what I expected. There was something on the inside of me that wanted to continue fighting and pushing through life like I always had, but at that moment a big part of me was just plain tired.

I was tired of feeling like I had been cast away. I was tired of being mistreated. I was tired of being the only one that was responsible for children that it took two to make, but I was the one holding their lives and future in every step that I made. I was tired of being beating by men. I was tired of having sex against my will, and being told that I should like it and shut up. I was just tired at that moment of living. But the one thing that I didn't expect was that mercy would fall on me and my child that night, and that God would send an angel to comfort me.

It seems that minutes did not go by after saying that prayer before a strange, peaceful rest overtook me on the floor. I found myself in a sleep so deep that I had never been in before, nor have I felt since that night. But while in that rest, I heard the voice of God telling me that "You can't fall off the floor. When you feel that you have gone as far down as you can go, you can either lie there, or get up." Then the voice said, "It's time for you to get up." Strangely, this was the first night that Courtney slept throughout the night. It had to be God!

When I woke up the next morning, I got up and looked in the mirror. I saw this stranger staring back at me with braids in her hair and looking shattered. However, I had this excitement on the inside of me that was ready to move mountains or die trying. I cut the braids from my hair, and decided that I was not going to cry one more day about the things that had happened to me prior to November 30, 1993.

That same day my counselor asked me what did I want to do with my life. Wow, up to that point I really did not feel that I had a choice in that. My father had always told me that I would never be anything. Society said that because I had children at an early age, I would only live in poverty all my life, and that I would pass that down to my children and their children. My mother never told me that Jehovah wanted to see me do better in life, or that he could help me do better. So why would I ever think that I could start to plan the course of my life?

However, Debra (my counselor) had a way of making me think that I could be anything that I wanted to be. So I took that day to think about what I wanted to do, and by the next day I had her answer.

I walked into her office before she could even put down her pocketbook and I told her, "I want my kids back; I want a house of my own; I want to go to school; and I need to find a daycare for my baby." She looked at me with a shine in her eyes that I had never seen anyone look at me with before. I knew that she could see something different in me because the first day she met me I was so depressed that I think I had a rain cloud following me. But I told her all my dreams with confidence and pride, like I knew I could do them all. She replied with, "Okay, I'm gonna help you."

I was finally taking responsibility for myself, my soul, and my children and it felt so good. Within days, we had completed my financial aid form, registered me in Savannah State College, and found a daycare provider for my baby. I started school in January.

By February of that year, Daniel was living with Ed and Mr. Reid, and my mother consented to taking Danielle into her home until I could move out of the shelter and find a place. The shelter would only allow you to stay for 120 days, and the day I left, I felt a little bit better because I had bought a car with my student loan money; I slept in the car most nights, when I didn't sleep at my friend Willa's house.

By May, when I had finally gotten accepted into the Section 8 housing program and found a house, I was ready to get my children back from my mom and Ed.

That July I moved into a Section 8 house. I was very happy that I did not have to take my kids to live in the projects. Mom gave me Danielle with no problem, and I found my happiness returning. However, it would soon be snatched again.

I had gone to Ed's house to visit Daniel several times before the day that would cause me to almost go to jail. The first couple of visits were fine. Daniel seemed to be growing fine, and I knew Mrs. Reid was feeding and loving him well. I would always tell her that I would have a house soon, and would be coming to get Daniel. She would encourage me and ask me if I was hungry or needed anything.

On a beautiful spring day, I rang the doorbell and she answered the door and said Daniel was not home. Though I felt it was strange, I left and returned the next day. On that day, I was again told that Daniel was not there. What was even stranger is that Mrs. Reid did not allow me to enter the house, and this Christian woman looked like she was lying. However, I left again with a gut feeling that something was just not right.

I drove to my parents' home that same day, only to find a very thick, important looking envelope waiting for me. My mother told me that a sheriff had made her sign for the envelope. It was from the Chatham County Superior Court's office. I opened it, and could not really understand what I was reading, but I saw the words… "We plead to grant sole custody of Daniel Stewart to Edwin G."

As I read the words over and over again, I felt like someone had kicked me in my chest. Immediately I realized that Edwin and Mr. Reid were trying to steal my child from me. The first call I made after crying for a little while was to Debra my counselor at Safe Shelter. She gave me the number to Legal Aide, and they set an appointment for me to meet with their legal staff the following Monday. However, I was determined that the weekend would not go by without me having my son at home with me.

I drove to Ed's house, and I was in female tiger attack mode as I rang the doorbell. As usual Mrs. Reid was moving slowly to open the door. When she opened the door I shouted, "Hey, where is Daniel?"

She murmured, "I don't know."

I could hear in her voice that was a lie, so I sharply replied, "What do you mean you don't know?"

She said, "You're not getting Daniel back! It's better for him to stay here."

Mrs. Reid had always been a very timid, soft spoken woman. I believe it was because Mr. Reid had a cocky, bossy, almost abusive personality. She is also the only person that I can say has looked like an old person all my life. I was never sure of her age because the slow way she walked in the house and the grannie gray wigs that she wore made me feel like she was at least 70 years old.

As her words broke through my ears and wrapped around my mind, I contemplated slapping her to the floor. I restrained myself because, though I was angry, I still had enough sense to know that I would cut my life short by being disrespectful to my elders. However, Edwin was fair game, and after I stormed past Mrs. Reid yelling, "I'm gonna get my son back!" I went in search of the "neighborhood crackhead," Edwin.

I don't know how many crackheads you have ever encountered, but catching up with one is very hard. Today you will find some that have cell phones, which makes them a little easier to locate. But I was trying to find that one in 1994 during the pager era, and he had already sold his pager!

I started my hunt with the usual hangout, which was the corner store where all the out of work men and drug dealers stood all day drinking beer, smoking and conducting drug transactions. Edwin was known to be there, but as my luck would have it, he was missing that day. Then I began going down the list of possible homeboys that he hung with. Each house that I went to turned up nothing. By then my anger had given way to panic, wondering if I would ever see my son again.

Just as I was feeling defeated and about to give up, I saw in the distance walking towards me the crackhead of the hour. He was easy to spot, because even on a dark street if you could not see his face, you couldn't miss that slew-footed walk. Both of his feet pointed outward, which left most people wondering how he could even walk.

I jumped out of my car and waited on him to get closer. As he was steps away, I screamed, "Edwin you sorry mutha fucker where is my son?"

He spit back sharply, "Bitch you better get out of my face!"

"I am not doing anything until I get Daniel." That is when he slapped me. The slap didn't even hurt because I was so angry. I turned to him and said, "If I don't get Daniel back this weekend, I am gonna pay someone to kill you, your sorry grandfather and your old ass grandma!"

He hit me once more for that but I was ready this time so I scratched him in his face and bit his neck until I tasted blood.

After the altercation was over I still didn't have my son, but I had a busted lip and a hand print on the side of my face. I also had an overwhelming desire to fulfill the promise of death that I had made.

A whole day passed since I confronted Edwin, but I still had Sunday to get through before I would meet with the lawyer that Legal Aide had me set to meet. I sat in bed that day wondering who could kill Ed without the heat coming back on me. The one person that I knew would do this for me without even thinking, I cared for to much too even ask him.

As the weekend was about to end, I made one more effort to somehow get Daniel. While driving on Victory Drive I saw a little boy running in the park. At first I thought my eyes were playing tricks on me, so I drove down and turned into the next entrance to Daffin Park. As I hurried to find the boys that I had just seen, I spotted Daniel. My heart was overjoyed. I got out of the car and hugged him. I held him close for a long time, and kept asking him if he was okay. Daniel seemed oblivious to the plan that Ed and his family had to steal him, so I didn't say much.

I just said, "Get in the car."

He questioned, "Where we going ma?"

"I'm taking you home with me."

After I arrived at the house I called Edwin to let them know that I had Daniel. Though I hated them for what they were doing to me, I did not want them worrying when Daniel did not show up at their house. I definitely didn't want the police to be called. Even though they called them anyway to report that I had kidnapped Daniel. However, the police told them that because it was civil and neither Ed nor I had papers declaring custody, there was nothing they could do.

Though I had gotten Daniel back, this was not the end of the war. It was only one of many battles that I would have to constantly fight for the next six months.

I remembered early that Monday morning that I had a meeting with the lawyer concerning those custody papers I had been served. I had never been in a lawyer's office before, but my time in college was teaching me how to speak and act professional! I had mastered public speaking so well that the Safe Shelter made me its spokesperson. Therefore, I was not intimidated by going to my lawyer for the first meeting. As I sat in the waiting area I knew only two things about my lawyer. One, her name was Karen Dove-Barr, and two she had good taste, because the waiting area was so classy.

When she walked into the room I saw that she was very tall, and lean. She had her blonde hair pulled into a ponytail, and wore a light green business suit like you would see on "Sex In The City," and she had a smile that released any fears that I may have had. She said, "Hi Mona , I'm Karen." She was nothing like the stuffy lawyers that you see on TV.

She escorted me to her office, and sat behind her desk. I was noticing that her office was just as nice as the waiting room. She opened a file that contained a copy of the papers that I had been served. As she took time reading all that Edwin wanted to do to me and my kids, she made little sounds that indicated she was really thinking.

Then she looked up at me and said, "Tell me about yourself?"

I started with, "I have three kids, and prior to moving into my current home, I was homeless and that is how Edwin was able to get Daniel." I ended my brief bio with, "I am currently enrolled at Savannah State University working on my degree in social work, and I have been on the Dean's list since I started."

Karen looked at me with a warm smile and said, "That's good that you were able to overcome your situation and now you're trying to put your family back together." Then she said, "Tell me about Edwin."

I started his bio by saying, "He is a high-school dropout, and a current crackhead." I ended with, "The only reason he wants custody is so that he can stop paying the $150 in child support for the kids."

Karen looked outraged. I didn't know if she reacted that way because a crackhead wanted custody of children, or if it was because he was only giving $150 a month to support two kids. However, with confidence she gave me her word that we were going to win our case. She told me that she would respond to the pleadings and all I had to do is show up for court after a date was set. Then she escorted me back to the lobby, and we said our goodbyes.

About five months went by before our case was placed on the docket for a judge to hear and make judgment. The first time we appeared, Edwin's lawyer asked for a continuance. This caused us a six-week delay from justice. However, the next court date came very quickly. As I walked confidently into the courtroom with my business suit on, I scanned the room for Edwin and Mr. Reid, but they were not there. I leaned over and whispered to Karen, "He is not here." I was upset because there were not many cases on the docket that day, so I thought that if he was not there, we would have to reschedule. I didn't realize that Karen had a trick up her sleeve.

When they called our case, Edwin's lawyer stood up to request a second continuation of the case. Karen was standing right beside him and she pulled out her polite attack claws when she said, "Your Honor, this would be the second time that this client has wasted the court's time. My client is a college student and she has to miss classes to be here. I am requesting that we proceed with judgment in this case." The judge asked Edwin's lawyer, "What is the reason for this extension, and where is your client?" His lawyer responded by saying, "Your Honor, I don't know where Mr. Green is. I have tried to make contact with him several times, but have had no success." The judge paused in his reply, looked at me and said, "I am comfortable proceeding with this case."

I didn't know what to expect since this was my first court case. Karen said, "Your Honor, we are requesting that Ms. Stewart be awarded full custody of Daniel and Danielle. We also request that child support be increased to $450 per month, and Mr. Greene be given visitation rights." Since there was no one to oppose our requests because his lawyer could not object with him not being there, it took the judge less than two minutes before saying, "So ordered, type it up as you stated and I will sign it."

Finally, the saga was over. I got more than I ever asked for, all because of Edwin! For many years after it was over I was tempted to tell him "Thank you for being an asshole, because it worked in my favor."

But nothing worth having is easy, and sometimes I felt that the God that I found in the shelter those many months before had left me and put a **"do not disturb"** sign on His door.

Continue reading and you will understand.

CHAPTER 4

God…Why This?!

I could never remember a time in my life that my sister Sherry was not my friend. Sherry was born with asthma, but she also had a heart for people. She had long jet black hair, and all of her facial features were slim, and she was a size 0 and never got over a size 5 in her life. She was sexy like a model, but the problem with that was that she was only 4ft 11in, so her modeling career would be limited to just family and close friends. Most of my life I looked at Sherry and wished I was more like her. She was dark like me, but so pretty. I always felt like the fat, ugly little sister.

Much like me, my father treated Sherry like she was the worst person in the world most times. As nice as she tried to be, and she didn't rebel much at all, my daddy would call her the bitch, slut, whore, and anything that would make that beautiful face fill with pain. Then she bore much of the beatings that the other children did, and sometimes she would perform just so that daddy could beat her more and the others that were waiting in line a little less. Because in our house when one child got a beating all of us had to, except Nikki because she was the baby and he loved her.

By the time Sherry was 16, she hated going to the Kingdom Hall. I remember her and my brother Mike talking about having to go to gatherings with other unfortunate Witness teens of that era. I am not sure how things are now, but during that time we could not associate ourselves with anyone that was not a Witness. So instead of Sherry being able to go to parties with her schoolmates, when she asked to go anywhere the answer was always "NO!" My fathers' reason for saying no had nothing to do with God, like I mentioned before my father was an Atheist. My father said "No" for two reasons, one was because he never wanted us to think that we could do anything that would bring us joy or fun, and two, because she was developing into a lady and I don't feel like he wanted her to be anywhere that boys were. So it was for these reasons that she never had the opportunity to play in the band, be a cheerleader, or even attend her junior and senior proms.

By the time Sherry turned seventeen and was in the 12th grade, the beatings were too much, and she had met her first real boyfriend and had run away from home. That was a very sad year for me, because up to that point Sherry was all that I had. I would come home to her everyday and talk about my day. She was the one that had comforted me when I was raped. She was the one that braided my hair and kept me in the hottest hairdos every ten days. She slept with me and kept the monsters away from my bed. She was my little world, and then my world was gone. It would be almost a year before I saw my sister again, because I don't know who was helping her hide, but they did a really good job. She had her own little "underground railroad" going in Savannah, with endless safe houses because everyone knew how mean and nasty my father could be to us.

After I didn't have Sherry to come home to, I found something else that comforted me in my home. I was playing in my oldest brothers' room one day, when I came across these books. From a normal view, you would think that he was just a serious magazine collector, but as I glanced at them I noticed that the similar theme to them was that naked women were on the front page. I knew that this was not natural, and at that point I had never seen a real naked woman. I saw the private parts of men, but their parts I associated with pain from being molested and raped. But it was something about the soft look of the women that I was looking at that caused me to think differently.

For many days and months I found the forbidden books being my pleasure and comfort. I lusted after these women that were only pictures on a page, but they were not a threat to me and in my mind they were soft, and they would love me. So just at the time when I should have been thinking about having a crush on a boy, I wanted no part of them. I wanted the softness of a woman. I knew that what I was thinking at this time was not right, because I had never seen a woman kiss a woman the way I wanted to. In fact, I had never seen a woman even hold hands with another woman in a loving way. Even though no one told me at age 13, that I should keep this a secret, I just knew I needed to. But even after having my first and second child, I still would look at women wanting and desiring them from afar.

Years passed, I was seventeen and still having these feelings, but Sherry was not there to give me advice, because for a season she had distanced herself from everyone in our family to focus on her new marriage and baby. So one day while riding in the car with my mother. I decided that I wanted to trust her with my secret.

I started by saying, "Ma, I really don't feel for men like I should." She didn't say anything, so I continued, "I really think that I like women, and I don't know what to do."

I didn't see my mother's face, because I made sure to stare out the window, but I could feel her fear and disappointment. The three minutes of silence in that car was deafening. Then she spoke and said, "You may have been hurt, but that is no reason to desire something like that, but you can never tell anyone about this." She could not even say the word "lesbian," and that was the end of the conversation. In her conversation with me, she never told me how to get past my feelings.

Okay, so I made another mental note that this is one of those keep for dear life secrets that you don't tell nobody. Especially because if one of our family members found out, or Jehovah forbid, one of the Witnesses found out; hell Mommy could have been disfellowshipped just because of me! So I tucked that secret under everything that I had ever done, thought, or been through, and hoped that it would go away if I did not act on it.

But do you think that the devil was gonna let me get away that easy? No! Even though I still kept the magazines as my comfort, and by this time I was old enough to buy movies that would give me more action and satisfy the desires that I did not know how to even began to satisfy with a fleshly woman, the seed that had been planted was growing, and the voices were getting louder within me.

At 22 I discovered the Internet and began using it as a tool to allow me to act on my desires in secret. Now don't get me wrong, there is nothing wrong or demonic about this wonderful tool, because it allows us to access information that used to take days or even months for us to receive. However, it will also allow a sick person to secretly be sick, and make contact with other people that have similar illnesses. I began to spend countless hours in chat-rooms talking to women that were bi-curious, black lesbians, lesbian moms, and lesbian wives. You name it; there was a title and a group that were welcoming me into their world. Finally, I felt like I had people that I could talk to, who understood my desires.

You knew it would not end in just harmless chat online right? I began seeking women to meet in person, most that had the same things to lose if we were ever found out. My desires finally got the best of me when I was 19 years old.

As I drove to her in the dark of night everything in me was nervous. I thought about turning around so many times, but I kept thinking of all of the books that I had looked at since I was 12 years old. In addition, all of the movies that I kept stashed in my closet were playing in my head, telling me that I had been waiting on this for a long time, and that I just needed to go for it.

So as I walked into her home, the fear was calmed after the second drink. Then came the moment that I had waited for ten years, when someone would kiss me with passion, and really wanting me. She told me that my body was beautiful, and that she would please me. I didn't know that this was my set up. I didn't know that as soon as her lips touched mine, and I touched her in that way that ignited passion of which my body had never known before, the windows of my soul were opened and every perverted demon that could rushed in, and they brought with them shame, guilt and depression as my parting gifts.

By the time I got home, I was asking myself "What have I done?" I had enjoyed something that I was told a whole nation had been destroyed for. That story was even in the Jehovah's Witness bible, so I knew that no matter where I went no one was going to tell me that what I was doing was the right thing. By this time Sherry and I were talking on a weekly or daily basis. She was very traditional in her thoughts and actions. I still trusted her with all of my secrets, but I knew that if I told her about my desires for women she would be disappointed, so I kept this from her.

Years would go by, and I had woman after woman that I could not love, because I did not want to become so attached that it would be hard for me to hide them when the time came, or if someone questioned our real friendship. I needed them only to provide that softness, and compassion that men had never been willing to offer to me. Some would find themselves falling in love with me, but that would end in tragedy for them when I disconnected from them without even a word of warning.

As the years went on, I would find myself in a heterosexual relationship only long enough to take a short break from women, or to see if I had actually started feeling like I could really care for a man. Every time I would give my body to male or female I would feel nasty and depressed. With a male I always felt their touch similar to putting lye on my skin, and trash in my mouth when they kissed me. Though many of them enjoyed me, I felt sick the next day, or even within that hour. Then when I performed with the many women that fell subject to my desires, I would only enjoy the act for the moments that it would endure, and I tried to make it last forever, because I knew the reality would soon hit me. That reality for me was that I knew what I was doing was wrong, but I felt I could not help my desires. I can remember so many days of loneliness and confusion, because of the way I felt for the women that I desired, and the men that I absolutely hated. I always had to drink plenty of alcohol in order to have sex with males or females. That's what led to my years of alcoholism.

By the middle of 1997, I had gotten tired of my secret life again, so I used my computer to find not a female this time, but a male. I think I must have put an ad out for the sorriest man that Charleston, South Carolina had to offer, because I found J. Somme. I liked him only because he was tall, and in his Coast Guard uniform, he actually looked like someone with some sense. I also liked the fact that he was away on the water a lot, so I would use his apartment as the meeting spot for the women I still had calling me. It saved me lots of money because though by this time I had been seeing women for about six years, I still never allowed any of my women friends to come to my house. Many of them didn't even know I had children. However, the last thing I ever wanted was for my children to see me kissing a woman. Forget the shame that it would have caused my mother, I thought about the confusion it would cause my kids. But sometimes I think that is caused them just as much confusion to watch me being physically and mentally abused by a man every time I entered into a relationship with one.

During that time I was going to college and really looking forward to the date fast approaching that I would be crossing that stage with my Bachelor's degree. I had already taken my LSAT, and scored high on it. I had talked to Sherry about my intentions to go to law school and she totally supported me. For the first time in my life I felt I was going to make my family proud of me. Wow, when I looked back and thought about the fact that three years prior to this time I was homeless with no job, and very little to want to live for. But now I was not only happy, but proud. This for me was a good place, seeing where I had come from.

Sherry and I chose Thursdays as our weekly chat day. I would either go to her job, or meet her at her house to discuss our dysfunctional family. I was also sewing a lot by then, and had a little part time job at the fabric store. It was December and I had begun a project that I had never done before. I had decided that instead of always sewing things for myself, my confidence had increased with my sewing talent, so instead of buying Sherry a meaningless gift this year, I was going to make her a red and black wool coat, with lining and all the fancy buttons. In my mind this was a coat that if I had to buy it, I could have easily paid $250 to $300 for. So I was determined to finish it by Christmas.

Christmas was a big deal to Sherry and me, because growing up we never had Christmas (well I never did, but Sherry had about 7 of them). She would go all out to make my niece Angie who was 15 feel like a princess, and that year Alicia would have been celebrating her second Christmas. She was 23 months old. Sherry had Joey (her husband) to install a new swing set in the back yard of the house they had just brought. She had just brought a new car, and she put a Christmas tree up that looked like a professional came in and decorated. So to me, except for the fact that my sister was battling a cold on that day, life was good for them.

Christmas Day arrived, and the kids and I stayed home. We had a good day, I just didn't have time to mingle because I was really trying to finish Sherrys' coat. The whole Christmas shopping season had caused me to be a little behind, but I told her that if I didn't have it by Christmas, I would have it by the 30th.

That day I remember calling my mom, and she told me that Sherry was not feeling well. I felt it was nothing serious because lately she had been a little sad, but she never would share with me what caused her to be sad. I felt it had something to do with her husband, because throughout the 13 years that they had been married, he had been on and off drugs. But she stood strong and took care of my nieces no matter what, and did not discuss her business with anyone. She was a lot like my mother in those respects. Sometimes she would tell me things that I had to read between the lines to figure out, but most times we were talking about how to fix my life. So even though I thought about calling her, I decided to let her rest.

Usually my gut tells me when things are about to happen, but in those 5 days after Christmas; I was too busy to listen to my gut. I was a member of a church that I was trying hard to keep appearances up for, and that was very hard since I was living dual lives. J. Somme was gone on the water again, and would not be returning until the 30th, so I took the time to "play" with some of my lady friends at his house. Then I was putting the final touches on the coat that I had 97% complete. I had fully intended to put all the buttons on the coat on the 30th. I also had a custom made label with my name on it that I was going to attach to the lining, so that it would look professional.

So on the 30th when my mom called me and said Joey had to take Sherry to the hospital, I went there just to see what was going on with her. When I entered the waiting area Sherry was in a wheelchair. My mom and Joey were right there with her. Sherry and I shared a joke like we usually did, and I asked her how she was feeling. She told me that she just felt weak. What was curious to me was that they could not get a pulse or blood pressure on her during that time, but because she was talking, they felt that she just needed some fluids. They diagnosed her with having the flu and being dehydrated and sent her home.

Well, my work was done, and I went back to J's place. He came in sometime that day, but shortly after greeting him, I got my second call from my mother that day. She called to tell me that Sherry had passed out, and Joey was taking her to her private doctor. Even though she worked at the hospital that we had taken her to earlier, we felt she would get better care going to a place that the waiting room was not running over with "emergency" patients who really had the flu.

I didn't go to the doctors' office to check on Sherry, I just felt it would all be okay. Hell, she was 34 years old, and except for being a sickly child, she had been okay for many years. By that evening I felt everything was okay, until my pager went off. It was Mom again. This time she was calling to say that they had admitted Sherry in the hospital. I rushed there. When I entered into her private room, Sherry was not laying at the head of the bed, but she was writhing all over it.

I kept asking her "Sherry how do you feel?"

And she said "Lisa, I don't feel bad, but I don't feel good. I can't get comfortable."

Then, I told her that "If the nurse comes in and sees you hanging off the bed, they are gonna think you are crazy and tie you down."

We both laughed. Then I asked her, "Where is Joey?"

She said, "He went home to get the girls ready for bed and will be back in the morning."

So that is when I told her, "We are gonna have a sleep over, just like when we were little girls!"

I was excited and could hardly wait, because it had been years since I had Sherry all to myself at night. In my mind we were gonna laugh and giggle til the doctor came in the morning and gave her some medication and discharged her.

J. Somme's house was five minutes from the hospital, and all I needed to do was run and get my pillow and some pj's, so as I put my shoes back on, and put on my jacket I said, "Girl, I will be back in a few minutes."

She said, "Okay".

My last words to her as I exited the room were, "I'll be back."

I walked downstairs to tell my friend Petra who worked in the medical records department that I was going to be in the room with Sherry all night. She and I stood there talking for no more than 6 minutes, and I left.

As I got off the elevator ten minutes later I could hear a very familiar voice, and I did not like how it sounded. It was my mother and she was letting out a sorrowful cry. My heart was racing because I saw nurses and attendants holding her back. She turned and her eyes caught mine, then she said the words that I had said many times working at that same hospital… "She coded! She coded!"

My mind could not wrap around this. I knew that most people that coded rarely came back. I had seen enough death on ICU as a nursing assistant and a secretary to know that lives changed forever on that floor.

However, I felt that God would not take her in the prime of her life.

She had two kids; my God she had a baby that had not fully started talking yet. She was married to her high-school sweetheart. She didn't drink, didn't smoke, didn't do drugs, and she went to church regularly. Everybody liked this quiet, beautiful lady. God was not going to let this happen was all I could set my mind on.

Several minutes after we had been in the family waiting room a doctor came to speak with us and gather information. Though, until that hour, none of the doctors that came in contact with her that day took her illness seriously, this doctor believed that she was going to recover. He admitted that they did not know what was wrong, but they felt that her age was going to benefit her.

Just after midnight on Dec 31 as I sat in the ICU family quiet room with my aunts, cousins, mother, and Joey, my mind was telling me that things would be okay, but my heart was aching like something tragic was about to happen. I was praying so hard.

In the silence, I felt the double doors when they open. I could hear sets of steps, and as the doctors approached. My head started to rush with blood, making me feel off balance, then they delivered the words that snatched my soul lose… "We did all that we could to save her, but she is gone."

I let out a cry that came from very deep inside, and even having to recall it to retell it to you now causes me to feel only a fraction of the pain, but I still know that it hurt so badly. All of my cousins tried to hold me, but I could not be consoled.

As they walked us into the ICU to see her, I must have moved on God's arm because my legs were not my own. There she lay with the white sheet pulled up, and her mouth was still a little open from when they forced the tube into her mouth. There she was, so fragile, so angelic. I know that they said that she was dead, but I searched her face for life. I laid my head on her chest because I wanted to feel her breathe again. Then as I raised my head up again and embraced her face in my hands, I looked down to see my protector, advocate, supporter, encourager, my sister, my best friend, and the keeper of all my heart-thoughts laying there lifeless.

I recalled our last words where I promised that I would be right back for her, and then the guilt set in. The devil infected my brain with the thought that if I would have never left her, she would have never left me. I had let her down, and I had no one to tell this pain to…my best friend was gone.

My mother sent me to deliver the news to Daddy. I drove into the driveway to my parent's home and went across the street to Victor and Michelle, who were our faithful neighbors and friends. Victor came to the door with sleep in his voice and his eyes, but when he looked in my face, he knew something had gone terribly wrong. I could hardly get the words out of my mouth before he embraced me, and I said "We have to go tell Daddy, Vick."

I was scared as I rang the doorbell and waited to hear my father's voice. My father opened the door for Victor and I, and with my tear filled eyes I said "Daddy, Sherry's gone, she's gone!" Daddy fell back, as if I punched him. He said, "What the hell?" He was dumfounded. I could not even respond, because I had no clear answers. Victor helped to steady him on his chair.

Then I saw a man that had never shown any emotion, other than anger, cry. The tears fell like water, and I realized that he truly loved Sherry. Our ride to the hospital was quiet. As I pulled up, I could see more of my family members had assembled. My Aunt Barbara took my father in a wheelchair to ICU and then to her room, where my mother was weeping bitterly. I watched as the parents that I felt mixed emotions for, held each other and shared the grief of knowing that the baby that they bore had gone without a days warning. Sadly that was also the only sign of affection I had ever seen them exchange.

The days leading up to the funeral were a blur for me. My brother Donald came home from being stationed in the Navy in Jacksonville, Ronald and Mike came from Atlanta, even Nikki blended with the family for that brief moment in time, and we grieved together. For the first time, our whole family was together. All of my aunts, uncles, and cousins gathered around us, and didn't let anyone come in to steal that time from us. For those few days, they even forgave my mother for being so deep in the Witness religion that she would not associate with them. Even in my grief, I was proud of how we came together. I wished I could freeze-frame those moments.

We buried Sherry across from one of her favorite restaurant on a cold January day. It was also her husbands' birthday. The only thing that I remember about the funeral is my brothers holding each other as the casket was being lowered into the ground. I remember my brother Donald, the Naval Captain, who was the strongest of us all, crying so hard that my brother Ronald had to hold him up and there I stood holding my kids. The sorrow from that day could have filled a mass of graves. I then carried that grief home with me, deep in my heart, to store with all the other hurts.

I don't actually know what happen after the funeral that day. I remember only days later when I walked into my sewing room, and hanging on the door in plastic was the red and black Christmas coat. I fell to the floor as I cried and begged God to tell me why He took my sister and friend. This sorrow was implanted firmly in my soul.

I didn't get an answer, and even if I did, I had no time to hear, because I had to return back to school for my last semester that week. I had to stuff my pain from losing Sherry down during the day because my last semester was an internship where I would be working in the county jail, and my hope was to land a job as a counselor in the jail after college.

I left the coat hanging on that door, but little did I know that thirty-two days from the day we buried Sherry, my life was going to change again.

On February 7th something on the inside of me, which had to be Gods spirit, told me to leave the house on that Sunday. The voice kept getting louder and louder with a sense of urgency that told me I had to leave. Even though I had already taken dinner out to cook, I told my daughter Danielle to put on her clothes and I looked at my mother, who had come to my house just to fuss, and told her I was leaving.

As Danielle and I ordered our food from Captain D's which was less than five minutes from my house, I sat down and wondered why I was buying food I could not actually afford when I had food at the house. But it felt good to have mother/daughter time without the other kids. Just as our food had been served, loud sirens from fire trucks, and police cars began to blare and passed the restaurant. Danielle looked at me and said, "Somebody's house is on fire!" I replied calmly, "Yeah, I hope they will be alright." Then we ate.

Riding back home was so peaceful that it took me off guard to see that my street was being blocked off by policemen and loads of emergency cars. As I approached, there was an officer standing in the street diverting cars. I rolled down the window and asked him how I was to access my house from where I was if the street was blocked. He asked me "Where do you live?" I told him "The first house on the corner." I heard him repeat what I had said. In that moment I saw the blood leave his face. His expression told me all that his mouth was unable to speak. Then, I vaguely remember him asking me to pull over.

As I jumped out of my car running towards my home that was surrounded by people, all I could do is think about my son Daniel who was supposed to be dropped off by his father that afternoon. I could not take another death.

It took about five men to hold me back from running into the burning house that I feared my son was in. Daniel had spent the weekend with Edwin, and he was supposed to be home at noon that day. Therefore, I thought that Daniel had come home and somehow set the house on fire.

I screamed in sorrow, praying that even if they found him burned, he would be alive. Neighbors were crying with me, and praying. Then came the news that pierced my heart, coming from a man that looked as if he was seven feet tall… "There's no one in there." I fell to the ground and just thanked God. Finally! Edwin had done something right by being late. My son Daniel had no idea that we had lost everything in the fire…but him.

The fire marshal informed me that the floor furnace had been old and faulty, and had exploded under the house. The entire middle part of the house was gone. If Danielle and I would have remained in the house there was no way we would have been able to escape. That night I went to church with my last $6 in my pocket and with smoky, dirty clothes on. I had no home, no clothes, and still I found the joy in it all, because in spite of what the devil tried to do, I praised God. My pastor prayed for me that night, and he announced what had happen to my children and I. By the end of that service I had $1026, furniture to fill another house, offers of rental homes, and I had witnessed the movement of God.

Two days later I returned to my internship. My instructors begged me to sit out that semester. They told me that I could graduate in the winter, but I was determined that I was going to graduate in June. And in spite of losing my sister to sudden death, my home to sudden fire, and being momentarily homeless, I still pushed to my mark, which was to graduate on June 2, 1998. And I did!

It was shortly after my graduation when I found out I was pregnant yet again. Yeah, I should have learned my lesson by now, but I took for granted that just because J. Somme was older and had no children, that he could not have children. I told him that I was pregnant the day after my graduation. Due to all the stress I had no idea that I was already three months along. However, J. wanted to make sure that I didn't get any further so that night as we slept in the bed together, he took the liberty of kicking me in my stomach, which was his failed attempt at causing me to miscarry.

I didn't miscarry, but I did cut him out of my life for the rest of the pregnancy. Not that he really wanted to be a part of my life anyway. But the feelings were totally mutual. After I delivered Sherry Kay on November 20, I called him to let him know that his first child had been born. He came to my hospital room, and peeked in like a stalker, then without touching Sherry, or saying a word, he left. That would be the last time I saw him prior to taking him to court five months later. I had already made up in my mind that I didn't need him to play a part in her life, because I was a college graduate, and I would provide for her myself.

It's a good thing that I did decide that, because for the next eleven years after her birth that sorry piece of work would call her less than twice a year, and treat her the same way he did the first day that she was born. However, I have consistently told her to forgive him, because I did not want any child of mine feeling hatred for their father (and I use that word loosely) the way I felt for mine. Hate and bitterness can kill you.

CHAPTER 5

What's a Three Letter Word for Distractions?
...MEN

Have you ever been approached by a man, and from the very first moment you felt that he has to be "The One?" Well, I don't totally hate men, but I never liked them either, so I have not had that feeling about men before. However, there are a few that have come into my life that I will never forget, but they all have taught me something either about life or about myself.

When I was 18 and pregnant with my third child I lived downstairs from the sweetest lady I had ever met, named Williemea. She was a single older lady and the mother of two kids. She would feed me and the kids most days because I had no income, but my mother had found that apartment for me and the kids. Even when she didn't have much to eat, she would share what she had with us. Then she would fill my heart with encouragement because I cried everyday.

If depression was my constant friend, misery was my pen-pal. Until the day my neighbors' nephew came to visit. His name was Greg, and he was 12 years my senior. He was so nice to me, always making me laugh even though, at 7 months pregnant, with two kids already, I had nothing worth laughing about.

Greg seemed to be the man that I had been looking for. He worked hard as a furniture and appliance delivery person. He made good money, and had no problem spending some of his money on me. About a month after meeting Greg, he moved into the apartment with me. He didn't seem to mind that I was pregnant. He didn't have any children. I was happy because he made sure we ate everyday, and he put air conditioning into our apartment so the kids and I could be comfortable. He also brought me a stove and refrigerator which I had lived without since the first day that my mother threw me and our bags full of clothes in there. I was so grateful to him. Here I was pregnant and had a man that told me how much he loved me everyday. I had no idea that the honeymoon would be over soon after I had my baby.

It was nearly August of 1989; I had still suffered postpartum depression even though I didn't have a baby to show for it. I had lost about 30 pounds, and only had enough energy to cook for the kids, have sex with Greg any night that he asked, and make sure the house was clean.

Greg would spend hours after work drinking in the living room with his friend, and I would find cut off straws all over my house when they left, but I never jumped to any conclusions. I was so young and naive that I had no idea to look for any warning signs.

I didn't mind Greg drinking because unlike my daddy, at least he would get up in the morning and work to help support my kids. I didn't have friends back then, and he was not happy if my mother happened to come over to check on us either. I didn't mind telling her not to come over because I got tired of her telling me how disappointed she was that I gave up my baby. That was just one less lecture I had to get if I stayed to myself. However, living a willful (or so I thought) life of isolation was really getting to me by the time I got my first job at the hospital about 4 months after having my baby.

I had been working at the hospital for about two weeks, when Sandra called and asked me if I wanted to go out and play cards with her and some other girls we had met at a cookout. I told her yes, and got dressed. I took the kids to the sitter, and left a note for Greg. I told him where I was, and who I was with, and signed it with a kiss.

Hours later I returned to the house to begin cooking dinner. When I entered the house Sandra was with me. She and Greg were almost the same age, and I had met her through him. It felt good when she would come over and hang out with Greg, Pete, and Van because then I would have someone to talk to while they were drinking. So that evening after she talked with Greg for a minute or so, she came in the kitchen to tell me she was leaving, and then I heard Greg close the door.

When Greg came back into the kitchen I looked up and the face that I saw was not the man that greeted me when I came in the door, and he definitely was not the man that I thought I had known for the past four months. His face was balled up, and his eyes were dark, and that is all I saw before his hand landed in my face, and the blood dripped from my tongue. He only stated, "You better never take your ass out of this house again unless I tell you that you can!"

I was paralyzed with fear. I thought to myself that even when Edwin was being a real ass, he would never hit me for nothing. All of our fights would be the result of arguments and me standing up to him. Never had I had any man other than my father hit me "just because." All that evening I was sad, hurt, and felt trapped. We were living together, and I didn't feel like I could make it on my own.

That night as I prepared for bed I was nervous and fearful of this man. After getting in the bed my stomach knotted up when Greg entered the room. He had been outside with the boys for hours. When he took off his clothes and got in the bed he moved close to me and said, "Bitch, you not speaking to me? You mad Bitch?" He was taunting me, and I felt it was nothing I could do.

During the weeks and months after that first hit, Greg would take any opportunity to dominate me. At lease once or twice a week he was either threatening me or beating me.

Even though Pete and Van knew that I did nothing to deserve the treatment that he gave me, they were too cowardly to stand up and tell him that a man should not hit someone that he claims he loves. His aunt, who was still my neighbor, would tell him that he should not be treating me that way. Everyone knew what he was doing, but they could not help me, because the only advice they gave was that I should leave, and I was not strong enough to do that.

I worked from 11-7 at the hospital, and had to walk most nights and mornings. The walk home was six miles long. Greg would call me by 8 every morning, and would be furious if I were not there to answer the phone. I knew that if I didn't meet all of his expectations, by 5 pm, we would be fighting. If I was at work and someone told him that I could not come to the phone, we would fight. If I stayed home sick from work, we would fight, because he thought I must have had someone in the house with me. He was accusing me of cheating so much, that sometimes it caused me to wonder if I was cheating on him and just not remembering it. However, at that point, I was not cheating on him.

This contemptuous relationship went on for another year before I found the strength to move on…the first time. I had taken all of his stuff to his mothers' house. I had cheated on him once or twice by this time, but with no one serious. I was just looking for someone that would treat me better than he was.

I felt that moving him out would mean the end of our little saga, because I even told him that I was going to get the law involved the next time he bothered me. Well, two weeks went by and I had not seen or heard from him. I was at a drive through window waiting to get food for the kids when I felt something that caused light to race to my head, and then everything went black. I thought I had been shot in the side of my head, but it was not a bullet that hit me, it was a brick. Greg had been stalking me, and used that moment when my guard was down to attack. It cost me twenty stitches on the side of my head and blurred sight for at least two weeks. But a nearly crushed skull does not teach you anything unless you want to learn.

After the attempted murder, he kept calling me telling me how sorry he was and how he wanted to make it all up to me. I was scared to go back, but hell I was scared to move forward also. It was 1991, and I had transferred my position from the 5th floor at Candler Hospital to ICU. I had gained more money doing a little less work, because I was not a nursing assistant anymore, now I was a unit secretary. I loved my job, and Greg knew it.

After allowing Greg to come back to the house I had to show him that I was not afraid to fight him back. He found this out the hard way though. One night we were invited to Van's house for a party. All evening Greg was bothering me and trying to start a fight. His constant drinking didn't help the situation. So as he came near me for what would be the final time that evening, I had a drink in my hand. I warned him to stop provoking me. That is when he took his drink and splashed it all over my white Addidas jogging suit. Before I could even think about my response I spotted a hammer that was on Van's counter top. I grabbed it and hit him in the head. I kept hitting him until I had plenty of blood to match the alcohol on my white suit. By the time the ambulance and police arrived, I was standing outside. With all the blood I had on me, they thought I was the victim. I don't even know how I got home that night, or how I avoided being arrested for attempted murder.

After he realized I would fight him back, I realized that he had a $300-a-week cocaine problem which explained the cut off straws in my living room and all over the back porch where he, Van, and the boys spent hours each night.

Soon after the hammer incident, Greg healed from his stitches and body wounds and started his abuse again. One night before I left for work, we had an argument. That night I had already decided that I was moving out with me and the kids again, and I didn't give a damn if I had to be on the street, I just wanted out. The fighting was beginning to show on me so much that I had developed permanent black eyes. So that night after leaving for work he called me at my job. I would not accept the call. I asked my co-workers to tell him that I was not available, and they did, until he had successfully placed his 110th call to the quiet ICU ward. I was more than embarrassed when I finally picked up the phone and said "Hello!" He said "Lisa, I am gonna mess you up if you don't come home now." I told him that I was not coming home. He said that he was going to get me fired, and I begged him to stop his foolishness because I was tired.

So by his 112th call I told him to meet me on 37th and Paulson. I left on my lunch break, and had no idea what was going to happen when I finally got to him. All I knew is that I had to get this nigga off me, and out of my life.

I saw his figure standing in the middle of the street as I turned the corner. I drove slow then stopped the car, and in an instant he reached in and tried to pull me out of the car. Well, at that point I did not know God, so luck was on my side that I was able to pull away and move the car. However, as I looked back at him something came over me that I will never forget. It was a combination of anger and hate as I looked at the man that was a threat to me and my sanity. It was 3 am, and the street was filled with just us. So in that moment I did the unthinkable. I turned my car around and pressed the gas peddle as hard as I could. My Ford LTD almost glided in midair as I sailed towards his 5'4 frame. Yep, I hit his ass so hard that he flew onto the windshield like a bug. Then I drove going 70 mph down the street with him holding on until I stopped, and he fell off onto the street. Then without even looking back I left him there for dead, the same way he had left me countless nights drinking my own blood as my children cried in their rooms.

I returned to work and the calls stopped. After getting home the next morning I turned on the T.V. to see if he was dead. He wasn't, and the only part of me that was relieved was the part that did not want to go to prison. The other part of me was ready to pack up and leave town.

The next day Brenda, the floor supervisor, called me at home and stated that she needed to see me in her office. I got dressed and met her there, and she stood there with her wide hips, and dark black face, telling me that she was told by the night shift staff that I had several phone calls coming into the unit that night. I told her the situation, and she was not moved at all. See you must understand that before Nichole Simpson got killed, the media, bosses, friends, etc...did not even acknowledge domestic violence. Hell, there are places in Georgia right now that will still tell a woman to suck it up, cause its "part of being with a man." However, Brenda who I thought would have understood my situation told me that I was fired. I begged Brenda that day to consider my children, but she looked at me as cold as she could and asked me to sign my termination slip. I was so depressed that, I really wanted to find Greg and kill him. After being fired I cut off all contact with Greg. Years went by before I saw him again.

I tend to forgive people that spitefully use me, and treat me like trash, but don't think for a second it does not make me feel a little better when I find out that the same people that were sitting in judgment looking down their noses at me get what they deserve. So years later when I moved back to Savannah and Brenda's ex-husband Michael was begging me to date him, it made me feel a little better knowing that for at least a little while she felt the hurt and pain that I did, when she fired me for merely being a victim of domestic violence.

Because I heard that he finally divorced her after cheating on her for many years. Oh, and in answer to your question… "NO, I did not go out on a date with him." But had it been the old me, not only would I have gone out on a date, I would also be living in that half million dollar house right now. As a matter of fact, I called her one day and told her how I forgave her for doing what she did.

Well, after Greg, I really didn't think that there would be another man. I made sure of that by going out with my old stand-by Corey. By then I was embracing my lesbian side. However, by 1994, I was in another real relationship with Marcus. I met Marcus through a close friend, and though he was shorter than I liked, he was funny and spent lots of time with me. I know they say you can't teach an old dog new tricks, but it would have seemed like I would have learned something from the years that I spent being abused by Greg. In fact I am not going to lie. Marcus did what we would call "full disclosure" within the first three weeks of me knowing him. He told me how he used to date a white woman, and how she betrayed him so he almost beat her to death. He told me how he spent time in prison for that incident. He told me that he was a now and then hustler and a wannabe pimp. Everything he said should have been the green light for me to speed on down the street. But searching for something you are lacking inside (love), will take you to places that you know good and damn well you should not go.

Being fully aware of his history, why was I shock the first time Marcus was violent with me? The better question is: "Why didn't I feel that I should leave?" Hell, I didn't even have to leave, because by then I had a house of my own. The rent and all the bills were in my name. I was getting all types of assistance from the State, and I was one of the few women I knew during that time that were getting child support on a regular basis from my children's father. Well, I will tell you why I didn't ask him to leave… low self-worth. It all boiled down to how I felt about myself.

I would be in the house, knowing that I didn't love this man, and my mind was already miles away from the abuse. However, something in me would always hear my father telling my mother that I "deserved" what I was getting. To me, if I could just not make him mad, keep the house clean, pay all the bills, provide him with the car that he drove, buy all the food, cook all the food, have sex with him on command, and if I had anything left, then I could go to school to better myself, so that he would be proud…then he would stop hitting me once a week, or whenever he was upset with the world. I figured then I would have paid my dues to have him love me.

I never took into consideration that this man had already told me who he was. He had shown me who he was also. Because my self-esteem had been reduced to the size of a flea, I really could not see that it was his problem and not mine. I could not realize that the bloody nose and the black eyes, and the ribs that-did-not-heal-well-from-the-last-beating-before-the-next-beating was a result of a man who did not care about me.

I was even praying during that time. I went to church every Wednesday, Friday, and Sunday. His uncle was my pastor. I would pray and ask God to make me a woman worth loving. I could not see that I was *already* a woman worth loving. I could not even see how all of this was affecting my children, who had to sit in their rooms at night, wondering when they were going to hear my frequent screams. I didn't know all the damage that I was doing to them, because all I wanted was to be loved.

Well, by the second year of our relationship, I had isolated myself from everyone and everything. I felt that if Marcus did not have a reason to suspect that I was cheating or that I was enjoying life without him, then the abuse would end. However, this theory had been a lie before, so what made me think that it would hold true this time?

It was the middle of summer, and I had finally had enough. I was praying, fasting, and reading in my bible every chance I could. I was trying to strengthen myself. I had even taken a break from women. I was able to finally tell Marcus that I was tired of being used. I was just tired of him period! So one night I told him that he had to leave. He was not happy about it, but to my shock he did not slap me to the floor. He did leave. I thought that it was finally over, and I could live again. Unfortunately, the devil had a plan for me two nights later.

I had told the kids good night for the 5th time, and I told Daniel if he got out of his bed one more time I was gonna beat him to sleep. Finally, he realized I meant what I said and went to sleep. I took my shower and decided to go to bed. I had unplugged the phone, because Marcus had been calling all day, and I was sure this time that we were not getting back together. I laid in my bed praying, but something just did not feel right. I had a wave of darkness flow over me that told me that danger was very near. I prayed and asked God to cover me and my children from all harm.

After finally falling asleep, only an hour had past before I heard my window shatter, and the window a/c was ripped from its resting place. Then before the scream could come from my lungs to my voice box a dark figure jumped through the window, and seemed to grab hold of me within seconds. All I heard was, "Bitch I'm gonna kill you!" I felt the cold hard metal of a sawed-off, double barrel shotgun on my temple. I grabbed at the barrel of the gun, and split my hand open trying to push it away. For an instant, my eyes locked into his, and I could see blood and darkness staring back into my begging eyes. It was like looking into the eyes of Satan. All I could do at that point is pray that my children would not be killed also, and that they would not have to see my mangled, lifeless body laying in a pool of blood. Then I heard the trigger pulled, I had a split second to prepare for death, and it was the longest of my life. All I could do is say "Jesus help me!" Then just when I thought I should be dead, I saw the look on his face as he realized that God was not going to allow him to kill me. The gun jammed. But it didn't keep him from hitting me with it instead. Then he left.

I was on the floor of my bedroom when it really hit me that I was still alive, and that my children would still have a mother in the morning, no matter how battered she was. I was going to be there. However, I did something that time that I had not done before. I called the police. Not only did I call the police, I had him arrested, and didn't drop the charges. I realized at that moment that this man was callous enough to want to take something from my children that he could never repay, and I was mad enough to take away his freedom. During that moment, I finally valued me!

For all the trouble that Marcus gave me, the courts merely gave him 18 month to serve, day for day. That provided me just enough time to get him all the way out of my system and move on with my life. His uncle and his mother who were my pastor and co-pastor were extremely upset with me. Their reaction did bother me, but I stood by my decision.

After the Marcus saga, I enrolled in graduate school to work on my Masters of public administration. Because I had been semi-single for a while I was having more encounters with women, and it was becoming harder to keep my lesbian life a secret. My younger cousins had grown up, and they were getting out more, so I had to be very careful not to be caught coming out of the strip clubs, or gay clubs that I often visited. I made sure that all the women I was going around town with looked feminine like me, and didn't try any stupid stuff like kissing me in public or holding my hand.

In 2000 I met a woman that caused me to think I could love her. We spent lots of time together, and she worked at a club where I hung out in. She was from NY and I loved her style. One day as we shopped in the mall, I was feeling good about life so much that when she stood close to me and kissed me in the mouth I didn't even move. But just as her lips released mine I saw one of my sister Nikki's friends, and panic rushed through my body.

Oh, my God! I thought long and hard about bribing the girl not to tell my sister, who I knew would tell my mother. Then I thought about leaving town, but I still had another year in graduate school. What could I do? So my answer was something that I did not want to do but the thought was there… get a man.

That is when Satan sent his second "son," Randy, who I called Big Dude. I had known of him since I was about 13 years old. I remember well the day that my brother Ronald broke Randy's shoulder blade playing tackle football.

However, back then he was a wannabe rapper, and would be on the radio station every morning as Pony Boy the Big MC. However, I was never into the hype of his celebrity, because I really thought he sounded stupid, most of the girls in our school just loved him.

It had been many years since I saw him or even heard his name, before the night that I saw him standing in the corner of the club. He was 245 pounds, and was so toned; you could eat off his washboard stomach. I was standing there in my leather outfit, thinking to myself "I know that man!" As I walked up to him, I called his "government" name (Randy) and he quickly responded by saying, "People don't call me that, they call me Pony." Then we talked for a little while.

The reason why it had been so long since I saw Randy was because he had been locked up in Florida. He did not go into detail, but I just figured it was drug related. I didn't think to investigate deeper, because to me he was a pretty nice person.

However, I did have many concerns because though he had only been back in Savannah a little while, he did not have any credit. His aunt had given him a car, and he was staying in one of his aunts' houses. Therefore, I felt he was having issues readjusting to being back in society.

He was strong willed, and we would sit and talk about some of the things that he wanted to do with his life. He told me that it was going to be hard to get a job because of his felony conviction, so I questioned him as to what he thought he could do to earn money. So he said that he wanted to drive trucks, and own a trucking company. I felt that was a good plan, and within 3 months he asked me to marry him.

I knew that I didn't love Big Dude, but I had never been married before nor proposed to. So I considered it for two reasons: one because he asked me, then the other reason was if I got married maybe I would not be a lesbian anymore. Yeah, I know that was silly, but I truly thought that being with him would diminish my desires for women.

I told him yes by November, and that is when everything began to change. I wanted our life to be perfect. I bought all new furniture in my name. I bought the wedding rings in my name. I got credit cards in my name. I brought him a whole new wardrobe. Then I helped him to get into school, because he told me that as soon as he got his first trucking job, we would be sitting pretty.

I didn't see any harm in believing him, because up to that point all I had shown him is that he could trust me to help him, so I figured that when he got straight he would make sure that all of my efforts were repaid. Besides that, we were getting married, and even if I was not in love with him, I still wanted our marriage to work. So we got married December 31, 2000. I chose this date because I wanted a happy memory to replace the anniversary of my sister's death. However, this day would become known as "The day that my credit died," so I would never celebrate New Years Eve again.

Things were fine between Big Dude and I until about two months after we got married, I discovered that he was seen driving women around in his car. I was upset when he came home, because up to this point I was making sure that he had no worries. He was in school, so all I wanted him to do was focus on that. However, when he came home that day I was furious and confronted him about my discovery. I was not scared of this almost-300-pound-man, but I should have been. Because no sooner than I told him that he was "sorry" and a couple of other choice word that is too harsh for this "PG" book, I felt my body go limp. Big Dude struck a blow that knocked me to the floor, and when I came to, I had no memory of what he hit me with.

I was very shocked that things went so badly, so quickly after saying "I do," but instead of calling it quits right then, we split for about three days. That was all the time I needed to mistakenly feel shame, a false shame that I was a failure at even keeping a sham of a marriage going for two measly months. This was also long enough for him to call me and tell me how sorry he was. From my past experiences, I knew that was a lie, but I just felt like maybe we could "pretend" for at least another year or so.

To me, I would not be successful in the marriage unless I could make it work for at least 3 years, but nothing in me loved this man. I was almost finished with graduate school, so after this incident my plan was to get a good job out of town and leave him anyway.

Well, all plans start with good intent, but as my Apostle Jefferson will tell you, "The path to Hell started with a good plan." The following week after he returned home, I began doing all that I could to keep him from getting upset. I found that to be a huge task, because I quickly discovered that this man was very jealous. Being a tall, massively large, abusive man coupled with jealousy is very dangerous.

He didn't want me to share his time with anyone, not even the three kids that I had living at home. Then there were the times that I would have to work late. That was always bad, because either he would come to my job and threaten me right there, or he would wait for me to come home and take off all of his rings before he beat me for not being home on time. My whole life was consumed with him, kids, work, and school, so I don't know why he was always accusing me of seeing someone else.

I wish the beatings were the only trauma that I had to endure from Big Dude. However, by the forth month of our marriage, I began wondering who I had really allowed into my home. At this point all I knew was this man was an abuser, a liar, and extremely jealous, but a simple search on the internet one

Thursday while I was at work turned up something so horrifying that I did not know what I was going to do. I typed in Randy M., and the Fla. Department of Corrections web page popped up. This website had much information to offer. My stomach began to turn as I waited for the page to load after I had once again typed in his name. As the page loaded the picture came first, then my eyes scanned the page, and in the "offenses" column was **HOMICIDE.** I must have stopped breathing at my desk for more than a minute. This nigga had killed someone, and now he was in my house with my kids…and I was now "Mrs. Murderer." My luck had gone from bad to worse!

Alright, I know that your wondering how that could have gotten pass me. To me when black men tell you that they have been to jail before, which he had, you don't really ever think "murder." Most times you think drugs, or guns, child support, or domestic violence. Hell, I don't know of any other murderer that is free walking the street. But this man had done this, and after seven years, his charges and conviction were reduced to manslaughter, so they gave him credit for time served, and let him out.

Okay, so how do you bring up the subject of your husband being a killer at the dinner table, or laying in bed during pillow talk? I didn't say anything that night, but my face and body language read like a book, but because all he could think of is other men when he felt I was "acting funny," we had a major blow up the next night, after I discovered I was "sleeping with the enemy."

We were sitting in the bedroom, and the kids were in bed, suddenly he reached out to touch me. Something in me did not want to be touched by this man, at all! Maybe it was the fact that anytime his voice went up in the house, I felt the pain for it. He would always tell me how much he loved me, but in my mind I wondered how the same hands that claimed this, could closed-fist punch me. As I flinched, I did not realize that I had moved away from him, until he grabbed me and threw me up into the wall. He asked me who else had been touching me, because that had to be the reason why I didn't want him to touch me. Then he told me that I needed to undress, as his hand was pressing my neck, and he was threatening to choke me. I was so scared, but I did as I was told.

After I undressed, he told me to get in bed. I did but was shaking. That is when he growled, "You better make it good!" I was like, "What?" He expected me to have sex? I could not put myself in the mood, but that would work against me, because since I would not willingly give myself to him, he would just take it. So as he ripped into me, and hurt me like only one man had done before, I mentally added to his wrap sheet "**RAPE.**"

After letting this animal know that I was afraid of him, and that his constant physical and sexual abuse was hurting me, it became more frequent. Sometimes the physical abuse would be accompanied with perverted sex. He seemed to only be able to perform sexually if he was taking it from me, or if he was allowed to talk about other men during sex. Yep, I said men! This big macho 300 plus pound man liked to fantasize about other men watching him have sex. Don't ask me what that was all about, but he also liked other things being done to him, which are too perverted for this book, but made me feel like he had gay tendencies. I know you understand!

Though I was deathly afraid of Big Dude, the day would come that I would have to make the choice of whether I feared him being there in my home more than I feared leaving him. He had already told me in our forth month of marriage that he could kill me and have a room full of alibis that could tell the jury that he was in the club when I was murdered. I believed every word that he said, and I desperately needed to find a way to ease my head out of this dinosaur's mouth. But this "man" (and I do use this word loosely, but again I am trying to channel my Apostle Jefferson into every chapter so I speak nicer), was about to turn up the heat on evil.

On the nights that Randy was not beating or raping me, I would have to drink a lot of alcohol in order to perform for him. The night of our final showdown started with me downing about four glasses of gin and juice to relax. Then looking at this mound of fat that was already laying in the bed looking like a beached whale, and reaching in the drawer to get the sex toy that he enjoyed being used on him more than a straight man should, but I did not mind using it because those were the times that I sought my secret revenge with the pain that I tried to inflict on him. After the first forty minutes of him fantasizing about different men watching him, this man said something that caused my "high" to go down quicker than ice cream melting on a stove.

Instead of continuing to disgust me with his normal perverseness, this man asked me what I would do if Danielle came in the room while we were doing what we were doing. Okay, let me bring you back up to speed, just in case you skipped a chapter. Danielle was my 13 year old daughter. Yeah, this nigger (Sorry Mr. Al Sharpton, I know that we retired this word, but sometimes there are no other words to use.) was fantasizing about my child! After I jumped up, I told this sorry SOB that he better never mention my child in any conversation! It took everything in me not to find a gun and kill this nigger. All I could think of was him trying to touch her, or raping her like he routinely did me.

That next day I started an argument that was sure to make him move out. It worked, and I didn't care how much he called and threatened me, I was not going back into that bondage. I was glad that I was able to protect my child, because I would not have been able to live with myself if I found out that the animal that I allowed into my home killed my daughter's innocence the way mine was murdered before I was even five years old.

By April, I was feeling free. I had started working more, and looking forward to graduating in less than one month. My boss, Anne, told me countless times that she was concerned about my estranged husband and his potential for violence. She had seen me with so many black eyes, busted lips, and choke marks in the past six months, that she could not relax knowing that he was truly gone. I should have heeded her constant warnings, because the devil had special plans for me.

It was the Friday before my big graduation day. I had worked hard for three years for this degree, and after the past six months of being in hell, I wanted school to just be over. Because as much stress as I was under from getting beat three to four times a week, I still managed to come out with a 3.6 G.P.A. Yep, I am pretty book smart! Then I had done so well during my internship with the City of Savannah that they wanted to keep me on full-time. So for me, in as sense, life was getting better.

The excitement of graduation was building, so on Friday night I had planned on going out with some of the other graduates. The town was buzzing, and there was a party everywhere that I turned because of so many people being in town for Savannah State University's graduation, which was always a big deal in Savannah. I was drinking, but pacing myself because I knew that I had to drive, and I did not want to be spending my weekend in jail for DUI. At 2 am I called it a night and headed home. I was smiling all the way home, and I was most happy that I did not bump into Randy while I was out. I had thought of it, because about two weeks prior to that night he had seen me walking with a friend of mine towards the club when he jumped out of his truck and beat me bloody in the street.

As I pulled up to my home, it looked quiet enough. I had learned to watch my surroundings because of the countless warnings that Anne had given me. As I walked into the garage and let down the garage door, I only caught a faint light. As I was walking towards the light I felt something hit me in my temple, right near my left eye. I saw a flash of light. Then I felt my flesh opened up, and the blood ran down my forehead. Everything was dark. As I fell to the floor, I felt a size 16 shoe, as it stomped on my chest, ribs, and face. Then I heard what I thought would be the last words I would ever hear, coming from the man that I thought I had broken free from. He barked, "I told you that I was gonna kill you, bitch." Then he left me, and I laid there wondering when I was going to die.

I don't remember anything other than waking up in the hospital. I remember police officers treating me like I was a criminal and not a victim. However, I was used to this, because even though it was 2001, domestic violence victims were still not being treated with the compassion they deserved.

Though I was in too much pain to sit up, I could tell by the way the nurses looked at me, that I was a mess. My jaw was swollen, but I managed to tell one of the nurses I was graduating on May 5th. She looked at me, and I could see in her eyes that she had no faith in me making it to my graduation. The total of my injuries were as follows: 30 stitches in my forehead, two black eyes, blurred vision from a concussion, busted lips, and 5 bruised ribs, which made breathing very hard. But, I was still alive.

I left the hospital against medical advice on the morning of my graduation. My first stop was Anne's house. Anne was, and still is my biggest motivator. She could bring reality to any situation, and I needed her to tell me why life was worth living at this point. When I walked into Anne's home, she looked at me and I could see the blood leave her face. "Oh Mona !" was all that she could say before welcoming me into her arms. I sat in her den, and she looked at me and said something so amazing that it sparked the fight in me. She reassured, "It was his intent to steal this day that you have worked so hard for, so you have to show him that he didn't take it from you. You must go to your graduation." She disappeared into another room, found me a pair of sunglasses and hugged me, and said "Go". Leaving her home, I felt empowered to go forward. I cried the entire distance driving to my home, but I made up my mind that I was not going to quit.

I put on my graduation garments, I positioned the cap so that it covered the stitches, and put on the sunglasses. The only thing that I could not put on was a smile. Even if my face was not so swollen that smiling hurt, I still didn't feel that I would have been able to find a smile.

As I stood there with all my classmates, my eyes were scanning the large gymnasium, looking for my family. I needed something to focus on so that I would have the strength to walk with confidence across the stage. The graduate students were always the first to receive their diplomas. They instructed us to stand and walk towards the stage. I prayed that I would not fall, and I made the walk with my children in mind. I wanted them to see why I worked so hard. I wanted them to see my strength, even though I was battered and bruised underneath. I wanted them to be proud of their mother. I took what I felt was a ten mile walk across the stage with my bruised ribs, and as my hand extended to President Carlton Brown, all of my fears went away.

Well, that was a great yet quiet undertaking for me. My family did not have a party for me. My aunts, uncles, or cousins didn't even attend the ceremony, but I could not focus on that. Immediately after the ceremony, my ribs told me that I needed to lie down. However, this was the amazing thing. At 6 pm. I was laying in my bed wondering how to live without breathing, because with every breath there was extreme pain. The evening news came on, and the second story of the evening was Savannah State University's graduation. As the reporter stated how many graduates there were that day, I looked and what did I see…Oh my God! I was on TV. In fact I was one of the only people that the station showed on TV, accepting a degree. They had my name up there and all!…graduate: Mona Lisa Black. Randy called about ten minutes later, and chuckled, "I'm glad you made it to your graduation." I replied in a very serious tone, "I will be happy when I attend your funeral." Then I hung up.

So the devil tried to steal my day, and had tried to take my life, but God! God set it up to where I could show the devil that he did not kill me. I still got up. I still walked. I still survived, and the devil could not take that from me!

Sidebar:

I was going to leave you wondering what happen to all of the male characters, but I feel that would be selfish to keep that to myself.

Well, it took many years, but I forgave Greg. He got fired from his high paying job because of his drug use. He began working for Van's family appliance business. In 2000 he began to show the results of all the years of drinking and drugs. He suffered from "wet brain," and after many years of chronic illness, he died at 47 years old.

Marcus got out of prison in 1998. We made our peace and he was even at the house the day I brought Kay home as a newborn. After that I would see him once or twice a year when I had time. He was no longer the mean, ugly man that I once knew. He became a person that I could talk to, and be honest with. I used him for several case studies in my graduate courses. He confessed to me in 2010 that he was so sorry for the things that he did to me, because he met a woman who for ten years dragged him like he dragged me.

And finally, Randy has swollen up to a whale-size 500+ pounds. He still drives trucks, but he never apologized to me for the things he did to me.

I don't hate him. In fact I have no feelings for him at all. It is as if he never existed.

All of these men taught me that getting into a relationship for the wrong reasons can only lead to hurt and pain. Also, trying to give someone more than you receive will leave you disappointed every time.

CHAPTER 6
My Hearts Desire

Nothing hurts more than to feel that you have been deceived or taken advantage of. But I feel it hurts 400% worse when you play an active role in your own deception.

When I made the decision to place Vandy up for adoption before she was born, a major factor in that decision was that the adoption would be open. I had never heard of open adoption prior to meeting with Jessica at the Parent and Child Development Center. I always viewed adoption as an event, where the mother was not allowed to see the baby. After she left the hospital she never saw that child again, unless they were lucky and Oprah or another talk show host reunited them after forty years.

This new concept of adoption was explained to me in great detail. Jessica told me all the perks of being able to choose the family that would take care of my baby. She promised that I would receive letters and pictures. She said that I would be able to talk, visit, and interact with my child as she grew up. I was so excited about being able to give my baby a good home filled with love. Then being able to give a woman that could not have children of her own a gift, is what I thought was the ultimate act of love.

I thought of my child growing up in a family with two parents, a dog, and near the best schools. However, as I flipped through the countless bios of all the potential adoptive parents, one stood out. It was the bio of a single black woman who was in the military. She had no children, but had made her career in the military. She stood out because I wanted Vandy to be with someone like me. I was a single mom, and though many people during that time felt that a single mother could not be a good mother, I believed that one could be just as effective, loving, and nurturing as a traditional set of parents. So I choose

Gloria as the adoptive parent for Vandy. For the first six months, I received a couple of letters from Gloria, and sent several. She sent me pictures of my baby, and I was amazed at how pretty she was. I slept with those pictures, dreaming of the day when Gloria would allow me to see her, or when she was old enough to talk and could call me Auntie Lisa. However, at about the 9th month I received a letter that sent chills up my spine.

This letter read like a good-bye letter. It started off by saying, "Vandy is doing very well, she is growing bigger each day. She has been crawling for a couple of months, and I feel she may walk soon." I was feeling warm and attached to her just through those words because I could see her in my mind. Then as my eyes continued to scan the page I read the words, "I hope that things will work out with you and your children. I wish you all the success in your life, good-bye." I looked on the back of the paper for more words. I needed it to be more than "good-bye". The picture she included in the letter was an Easter picture of Vandy, and it was the last one that I would ever receive.

I did not get alarmed in the first month. Even the second month went by, and I only vaguely realized that my letters were not receiving a reply, but I did not allow panic to overtake me.

After six months of not hearing anything I sent a letter to the adoption agency. I found out Jessica had resigned, so I had to talk to other people about the situation. Each person told me that they were going to send my letter to the adoptive parent. They said that I would have to wait for a response. That response never came. It hit me when a year had gone by without a word that these people had allowed this woman to steal my baby. You may not realize it, but in any adoption, a mother has one year before the adoption is final. During that time I could have told them I wanted Vandy back, or the baby's father could have come and told them that he wanted his child, and by law, she would have to be returned. However, she didn't set the alarm off until the ninth month of her already-well-devised plan. By the time I reacted, it was already too late, and I believe Gloria knew this the whole time.

I would cry every time I thought of Vandy, for the first 6 years. I could not talk to my mother about my feelings, or anyone else for that matter because adoption was not popular in the black community, I just felt people would have thought that I deserved to feel like that for having the nerve to give up my baby. In fact, I know that my mother felt that way. Sometimes, I would call my Aunt Barbra, because she never judged me. She would pray for the healing of my mind, and for the hurt that I needed to be removed. However, only the loads of alcohol that I consumed during my quiet hours ever numbed me from the pain. However, when I would sober up, pain would still be there.

On Vandy's 8th birthday, I cried until I was sick to my stomach. I made up my mind soon after that day to pretend that she did not exist. I did just that for the next 10 years. This was not a foolproof plan, but it did stop the dreams. I set 10 years as a measure of time because I read that I could begin looking for her when she turned 18. I suppressed this memory into the same area of my brain that stored my rape, molestation, and years of abuse.

Five years passed without me even thinking about Vandy and the whole ugly situation. However, by the sixth year I was reminded about her by my best friend Claudia. Claudia and I met when I was 19 and working at the hospital. She worked there also. We found instant friendship because we were so much alike, but different enough to compliment one other. I often balanced my heart between her and Sherry. I found that I could tell Claudia everything that I could not share with Sherry. That's why she was the only person that I saw daily, who had access to my parents that I trusted to tell I was a lesbian.

She never judged me, and no matter what I told her, she would look at me and say "Oh, really?" Then we would transition to the next subject.

I honestly knew that if I ever killed someone and needed to hide the body, she would devise the plan, dig the hole, bury the body, and we would never say another word about what happened. That's the kind of friend she is.

So after Sherry died, she became my sister/friend. I spent countless hours on her couch of confession. One day as we sat talking about the issues of our hearts, she said "Hey, have you heard from Vandy?" I paused as my mood saddened and said, "No." Then the tears that I found no strength to hold back began to fall.

She said, "What's wrong?" Then I started my confession with, "They stole her." She looked confused and then jumped into fight mode as she questioned, "What, Who?"

Though Claudia knew about Vandy and her birth, until that day she never knew that I was holding back that pain. Sometimes after the first year we would talk and I would become very sad. I think she felt it was guilt, and I never said anything differently. Then, because of her bond with me she stopped bringing up the subject of Vandy. So on this day I felt compelled to tell her the whole story. She hugged me as I finished my confession and we both cried endlessly that day.

After leaving Claudia's house I went home and took out Vandy's pictures. For the next five years I would look at the pictures on Thanksgiving, her birthday, and Mother's Day. I prayed during those moments that she had a good life, and I also prayed that the person that stole her from me would find some compassion before she turned 18, and let me know that she was still alive. I was tormented by the thoughts of my baby being abused, or not happy.

By 2004, I was 34 years old, in a good career with the State of Georgia. Moving to Cordele right after graduate school allowed me to finally start over in a new life. I had come to a job making more money than I ever expected to make in my entire life. I was living in a very nice townhouse. I was finally enjoying life because I was free to be a secret lesbian without fearing that my family would find out. I still did not want to come out of the closet, because by then my children were old enough to know exactly what was going on, and I did not want them to see a side of me that I was not proud of. So I would go to the many neighboring towns when I wanted to let my hair down. I had plenty to choose from, so Albany, Macon, Warner Robins and Atlanta were my creeping spots.

With all the positive things that were going on in my life, I still had a feeling of emptiness. By then enough time had passed where I could look back on the long journey that I had taken to get to success, and I realized that even though I had children, I had never really been able to be a mother. I didn't feel that I would ever meet a man, fall in love, buy a house and put a dog in the back yard. However, the one thing that I did desire was another baby.

I had prayed and asked God for a little boy. Don't be upset with me, but though I had delivered four girls, I always desired to have a house full of boys. I think I secretly felt that I could raise them up to always protect me, the way my father and brothers never did. Giving birth to Daniel, as my first child, gave me hope that if I got pregnant again I would have another little boy. However, Danielle broke my hope. Then Vandy, Courtney, and Sherry diminished even the dream of one day having a boy. Until the day I laid eyes on Curtis.

Curtis was the youngest boy of 6 kids, and four of his siblings were boys. Each time I went into the store where he worked part-time, I would catch him looking at me. Within months I became a regular at this store, and I had a mutual attraction to him, but neither one of us were willing to break the tension until Valentines night 2004.

It must have gotten too hard for him to resist by this time, because he ran out of the store behind me, as I was getting in the car to open my first beer for the evening. By this time, I found out why people would often times tell me that I was just like my daddy, because I was a functional in the closet alcoholic. Most nights I would get home, and if I did not have to cook, I would go to the store, get a six pack and a pint of Remy, and then drink until I passed out.

This night was different. As he approached me he asked, "Hey can I have your number?" I just looked at him for a second, as I asked in my proper English, "What is your name?" Then he realized that he never even asked my name, so he said "My name is Curtis, what is yours?" I said, "My name is

Mona." Then he stated, "You're not from here are you?" I said, "No, I'm from Savannah." Then after that one-minute exchange, he asked for my number again. This time I looked at him kindly because since I had been living in Cordele he was the only man that had ever asked me for my number or even talked to me. So I gave him my business card, and put my cell-phone number on the back. Then I went to see my girlfriend who was waiting at the hotel for one of our weekly rendezvous.

Curtis didn't call me that night, or even the day after. He emailed me at work about a week later. From the very first email he was funny and very charming. I told him who I was, and that I was not looking for a man. He was a little shocked because he said that by looking at me, he never would have thought that I would be a lesbian. After emailing each other everyday, all day, for weeks, we had our first date. Our dates were mostly him coming to my house and watching TV with me. That was fun, because up until that time, I had not had any company at home.

Curtis did not mind me being a lesbian; in fact he encouraged me to be who I was. He would often tell me that I should not have to hide my life. But Curtis grew up in the same cult of Jehovah's Witnesses that I did, so he knew what I was up against if I went astray.

It was very natural that this man became my best friend. He was the only man I had ever met at that point in my life that I truly enjoyed spending lots of time with. He enjoyed laying on my bed and listening to stories from my Lesbian Erotica book. He was intrigued as we engaged in conversations about life. He saw me as strong and independent.

It seemed like a month had gone by before the subject of sex came up. After safely escaping Randy and moving to this little town, I made it my life goal to never be with another man sexually or otherwise. I had gone a whole eighteen months without sex with a male, and in my mind I felt I wasn't missing a thing.

So, on the night that Curtis and I were doing our usual talking, listening to music, and drinking, he kissed me. It wasn't electric or mind blowing. It was just a kiss. However, that kiss turned into him pulling me close and promising me, God, and all the disciples that he was going to be gentle and not hurt me. He even told me that he had fallen in love with me. I felt that was dangerous, but I regarded it as a statement that most men used to get what they wanted. However, I was curious about what it would feel like to sleep with my best friend, so I consented.

Well, because it had been so long since I had sex with a man, he could not keep his promise of not hurting me. However, he kept talking in my ear the sweetest words a man had ever shared with me to steer me through the pain, and into a pleasure that I had only dreamed of.

After that first night we shared a very special love life. It was more important for us to be friends, than to be together sexually. All he really wanted was for me was happiness, and pleasure. For this reason, when I told him one night as we were lying in the bed that I wanted a baby, he did not jump up and run. He looked me in my eyes and asked, "Why?" I told him how young I was when I began to have children, and how I never really felt that I enjoyed any of my kids growing up because I was always in crisis mode trying to survive. I also told him my desire for a little boy. Then he asked me, "Why would you choose me?" I replied, "Because you're my friend."

However, there were more reasons: he was 5'11, with Hersey's Chocolate dark skin, a husky football player build with broad shoulders and a thick neck, legs like a runner, a butt that made any pair of jeans look good, curly black thick hair, perfect lips, brown eyes, and to enhance things if I had a boy; Curtis was blessed and highly favored in the male anatomy department. He was also smart, because he was a math and history major in college. Those were two of my worse subjects. Therefore, I felt confident he would pass these good attributes down to my baby. The only thing that I didn't want him passing down was his freakish clown nose. His nose threw off the harmony of his face the same way Michael Jackson's did to his. However, if this was not a flaw, he would be perfect, and God did not make any of us perfect. Also, if you love someone you look past their flaws and see perfection. Though I did not see perfection when I looked at him, I did see a face that I could wake up to every morning, a face that I did not mind passing down to another generation.

So after I explained to him all the reasons why we should have a baby, he climbed back on me for another three hours, which gave me lots of time to know that he was a good choice.

About six weeks later I found out I was pregnant. I was so happy. Curtis was happy also, even though our life was filled with scandal. Because Curtis was still married and the whole town knew about us. But all I cared about was the fact that we were best friends and having a baby.

We never talked about each other as being a couple. He was my homeboy, and I was the coolest woman that he had ever encountered. We would go to strip clubs together, and even though he could not dance a lick, he would also take me dancing. One evening as we got ready to take a shower together, something happened. I had just been to the doctor that day, and saw my little bean on the monitor. It was confirmed that there was a baby on board, and I was excitedly talking to Curtis about it. However, as I stood in the shower waiting on Curtis to get in, I saw blood streaming down my leg. I didn't feel any pain, but I felt faint from seeing the blood. I called out to Curtis in a panicky voice, and he ran to me. I saw the look on his face, and I knew that this was not good at all. In total silence I got out of the shower and dried off. We laid there holding each other. I did not want to go to the hospital, trying to delay confirmation of what I already knew.

We miscarried about two days later, and to finalize this, I had to undergo a D and C. I was so depressed. For weeks, not even my best friend Curtis could bring a smile to my face. In six weeks, I had lost so much weight that my clothes were just hanging off of me. By October, Curtis believed that the only thing that was going to help me was a vacation, so I prepared to go to Jamaica to renew myself.

Even though Curtis and I were going through this very rough time in our friendship, it did not stop us from eating lunch together everyday. My sex drive was non existent. I had even stopped seeing my secret girlfriend, whom Curtis actually knew about. He was so worried about me that he would insist that I call her and hang out with her. I would lie and tell him that she did not answer the phone, or that she was busy knowing that I had never even tried to contact her. He felt that if I got back in touch with my lesbian side I would suddenly forget the pain of my lost. I realized that men are so simple in that way. He didn't understand my inner struggles. However, the day before I left for my cruise, Curtis and I sealed our friendship with our passion for each other.

By the time I returned home from my vacation, I was feeling good and renewed. My body was feeling different. Strangely enough, I felt pregnant. I was pregnant, and this baby if I could help it, would not be going anywhere! I rested as much as I could, but seemed busier with work than ever before. I lost weight the first few months but the doctor was not concerned. She begged me to eat as much as possible. I was still praying for my little boy, and the first week in March, they told me that my prayers were answered. However, my worse fears were realized in that same day. They told me that I was having a little boy, but they feared that he had Downs Syndrome.

The doctor asked me if I wanted to end the pregnancy. Even though my baby was not coming to a married couple, I did not feel that God would answer my prayer with something so hurtful. I would not accept what they had spoken over my baby. In fact I told Curtis what the doctor said, but I would not tell anyone else. I did not want people cursing my child before he even got here. I just kept praying for a normal child. I told God if He gave him to me, then I would give him back. I made every promise to God that I could as a bargain for my child.

Though I thought this would be the happiest pregnancy I ever had, it turned out to be far different. In addition to having to worry about the baby on the inside, I had to worry about the drama on the outside that seemed to be mounting.

Curtis's wife had begun stalking us, so I never knew when or where she was going to turn her "crazy" on. According to her, I was "public enemy number one" because of our relationship. My job was going through management changes, so we lost my favorite executive director, and they replaced him with a male that I suspected of being gay.

Then some of my children were very upset because they did not want me to have another baby. Daniel called me from across the country to say "Mama, how could you be having another boy? I was supposed to be the only boy!" Okay, this big hard grown man was on my phone whining about not wanting another boy to be added to his sibling list. Kay, my youngest girl, didn't care if it were a girl or boy, but she didn't want a baby in the house at all! Danielle was my only friend. She never said anything about the baby. She stood by my side and catered to me the entire pregnancy.

She was even at the doctor with me the day I found out that I was having a little boy. Each time I went to the doctor's office, which were move frequent due to my age and complications, I maintained my focus on having a healthy and strong baby. This was my first pregnancy where I had lots of money to spend. After I would leave the doctors' office each week, I would spend lots of time and money in Babies R Us, Marshall's, Baby Gap, Punch & Judy and every baby boutique I could find. I spent more than two thousand dollars on clothes, one thousand on baby furniture, nursery decorations, and toys. I brought so much for this baby that it didn't even bother me this time that no one threw me a baby shower. Hell, you can't miss what you never had.

The night before I was scheduled to go into the hospital I was stressed out. Because I had purchased all the items to design the nursery, but none of his furniture had been assembled. This was Curtis's only job during this pregnancy, aside from staying out of my way. I expected him to do this during the last three months of my pregnancy. However, by the end of my pregnancy when I stop wanting to have sex with him, it seemed like he really got off on pissing me off. Everything I requested he would either challenge me, or he took his time completing.

He had many baby-like tantrums when I would withhold my affection. He didn't realize the danger of what he was doing, but he received the reaction he was searching for when I would stand back on my already bowed legs, and give him the cussing out that his wife never would. I gave him three a week just to make him feel like I was paying attention to him.

So the day before delivery when my mind was racing and hormones raging, I had to call Curtis. He answered the phone "What," like I was bothering him. I replied, "Boy, don't what me! When are you coming to get the room together?" He responded dryly, "Lisa, didn't I tell you that I am going to put the stuff together? So why are you tripping?

I exclaimed, "Curtis, your only freaking job this whole time is to do this one thing for me, so why are you playing with me?" He sharply said, "Well with your attitude, I may do it or I may not." Then he hung up the phone. I was pissed. No, I was past pissed because I was nine months pregnant, and I knew Curtis was just acting that way because he could, and there was nothing I could do about it. However, he didn't know me well because I was about to show him the other side of me.

Hours went by, and I had not heard a word from Curtis. Suddenly I heard my front door open, and footsteps charging up the stairs. The steps stopped at my room door and then it opened. "Hey baby", is what Curtis said in a cheerful voice, like he didn't piss me off and hang up the phone in my face. Just as he smiled at me, I snapped. I leaped off the bed, as if flying through the air and landed right on him, kicking, slapping, scratching and punching. I was so angry that I felt like I had super human strength. He tried to hold me, because Curtis was the type of man that would rather die than to hit a woman, but he had no problem saying slick things out of his mouth. However he couldn't even hold me.

When he realized that I had been pushed too far, he began to shower me with "I'm sorry baby. I'm sorry." I could care less at that point because I had seven months worth of stress on my chest. I had endured it all with my head up high, even when I wanted to go somewhere and die. All I wanted in return was a peaceful night before my delivery, and since he was not willing to give me that, I was going to make him feel it.

After I tired myself out, and Curtis rocked me in his arms trying to quiet my crying by telling me how sorry he was. He did this for about an hour, and left me falling asleep on the bed. About thirty minutes later he and his older brother Kent came back to my house and put together all of the furniture. I was happy finally. But I ended the night by telling Curtis, who I was still upset with, that I did not want him in the delivery room with me that next day, and that his services were complete.

On the day that he was born, Danielle sat in the operating room waiting on his grand entrance, as Curtis and others waited outside. When they announced that he was here, all I could do is ask Danielle how he looked, over and over again. I knew that if he was a Downs baby, even she would know that something was wrong. She told me that he was OK. They allowed me to see him, and he was perfect. Dallas Scott Andrew did not have Downs, and thank the Lord, no Curtis nose!

But months after his birth they discovered that he was born with a bone disease, which shook me to my soul. This disease would consume my life for the next two years. Doctors told me that it was unlikely that he would walk, or talk at the time when most kids did. In addition to the bone disease, he was what you called delayed. I stopped working, and poured myself into getting him well. By this time I was also dealing with the knowledge that Curtis, my best friend and lover was battling colon cancer. Yeah, my life was going down really fast, really quick. I found that bad can get worse.

Alarms in Cordele would blare very loud during the days when the clouds are very dark to signal a storm coming. The alarms only sound when the storm is becoming intense and they tell us that how we view this simple rain storm needs to change. So, I often wonder why when real change is coming in our lives alarms never ring. It comes without warning, and most times in my experience it is not the rainbow, it's usually a hurricane.

Things were indeed changing because it had been months since I had been home. I was dealing with both Dallas and Curtis being sick, no job, and the money that I had saved was running out. My travel was limited.

However, September 8, 2007 was significant for me because that day I was in Savannah and it was Danielle's birthday. It was a good day for me, because Edwin and I were finally getting along. He allowed me to plan for a party at his house for Danielle.

As I was running from store to store, and calling Ed every twenty minutes to remind him not to forget different party needs, I realized he and I were actually communicating kindly with each other.

I found on that day that I had forgiven him for every time that he lied to our children and caused them pain. I forgave him for living not even twenty houses away from me and his only two children, and many months went by that I had to beg him to come and see the kids. I had forgiven him for taking care of children that did not belong to him, and the two that he knew belonged to him, he turned his back on and closed his doors to. I forgave him for all the Christmas, birthdays, and Father's Days when I had to look into my children sad eyes and lie. I had to tell them that he loved them, even though I knew that real love would not let any time, space, person, or thing separate him from his children. On that day I knew that God had changed me, but still I had no idea that my life was about to change.

We were sitting playing cards, eating crabs, and acting like a real family when the phone rang. It was my mother's voice on the other end telling me that we needed to get home because something was wrong with my father. It took a few seconds to process my thoughts, but when I did, my gut told me what my mom could not—he's dead.

The ride from Ed's house to my parent's home took ten minutes. My mind could not be in those moments because all I could do is think of the last time my father and I really had a conversation. It was March 2007, about 6 months before this day. I had made one of my infrequent calls to my parent's home, because it was going on a month since I last spoke with my mother. I tried to keep it like that because it gave her less opportunity to ask me for money. The phone rang and to my surprise my father answered the phone.

I knew the moment that I heard his voice that my mother was not at home, because my father NEVER answered the phone if he did not have to.

My father was a very social person but like many men of his era, he was not a phone person. So when he said "Hey girl"

I replied "Hey daddy, where's mommy?"

"She went to one of those damn conventions with them people."

"Well how are you enjoying your peace and quiet?"

"It's Good."

So instead of saying good-bye, I engaged in more conversation with him.

"So what are you doing" I asked.

"Nothing, just watching a little news, these crazy ass people are down here breaking into people houses and getting killed." Then he said, "So you getting ready for Nikki's wedding?"

I laughed and said, "That's just a mess! Why is she marrying this nigga? It's like she has a "stupid" sign painted on her. And why is she having a big wedding? She can't afford it, and I can think of 1000 other things that she can stiff mommy out of money for." Then daddy laughed and I knew he just wanted to pick fun at Nikki.

Then daddy asked, "Lisa, you still have not found a job yet?"

I felt sad in that moment; because I knew I had been hiding many things from my family. I responded by saying "No dad, its hard to find anything right now. I have sent out more than 100 resumes and only got two interviews, and no job. I tried."

"It seems like with all that education you have, you would be able to find something."

"Yeah."

He said consolingly, "You'll find something."

"I hope so." Then just as we were about to end this 27 minute phone call he said something that changed my life. He said, "I love you girl."

I paused and said "I love you too daddy."

In all of my 37 years, my daddy had called me many things. He had said so many ugly things to me and even beating me severely, but the one thing he had never done or said is that I was loved. In that moment he told me that he loved me. He loved ME! I was validated, and finally worth loving. I wanted to freeze that moment forever, and play it on the days when I was feeling unloved. I almost cried because it was so touching. I wanted him to repeat it a million more times. I wanted to be near him, and feel his hug and see his smile the next time he told me he loved me. He had finally fulfilled one of my hearts desires, and he didn't even know it.

The ten minute ride came to an end and I jumped out the car. I ran to the ambulance that was making no haste to leave. I saw the medics working on him in the ambulance. I looked at the man that I forgave for a lifetime of hurt, and I didn't want him to leave me before I made him proud. I wanted him to know that his little girl was going to be someone great one day.

We drove behind the ambulance to the hospital and sat in the family waiting room for the doctor to visit with the status report. When the door opened a doctor stood there and spoke the words that my heart already knew. He had a massive heart attack and he was dead.

They prepared him so that we could see him one last time, just as we had done Sherry 10 years before. Walking into that room was hard because I knew this would be the last time I touched my father's warm body. Though I knew he could not talk back, I still believed that his spirit was close to his body. I spilled my heart to him. I begged him not to leave until he saw my end, but in that moment I heard him say to my heart "I know you will be okay, and yes, you are worth loving."

After my father's funeral I returned to Cordele, still depressed. I was looking forward to the following year, because Vandy was going to be turning 18. Finally I was going to be able to find my child. *So I thought.* Unfortunately, I would be delivered news that would break my heart shortly after I contacted Parent and Child Development for the first time in nearly 11 years.

I received a letter from the agency in November. It stated that in Georgia I could not even begin my search for her until she was 21, and that they were going to charge me $300 to assist. I fell on the couch and began to cry so hard. I had waited all this time, only to have my hopes put off for another three years, and the people responsible for my child being missing are going to charge me money that I did not have in order to find her. I called my Aunt Barbra, and just cried to her. I think she must have prayed, but not while I was on the phone.

I could not allow that news to keep me down, because I had a sick child that needed me. By this time Dallas was two years old, but still not walking or talking. I had him going to physical therapy, and speech therapy. I was praying, and asking God to heal my baby. He was two, but he looked like a 10 month old baby. However, a miracle was about to happen, because God was going to answer my hearts desire once again.

One day as Dallas scooted around on the floor; he pushed up and stood in the middle of the floor. Then he took the steps that I had prayed for. That one step turned to two, and by the weekend he was running all over the house. Curtis and I were so excited. Then about one year later, he would begin speaking. Now at 4 years old, I can't shut him up, and he won't stop running in my house. Each day when I find myself wanting to be upset with him, I stop and think on all the things that the doctors had spoken over his life, and then I think about how God blessed him and healed him. His disease went into remission July of 2009.

Well, December 3, 2009 started off like every other hurried day. I moved back to Savannah in 2008 to help my mother, who was still dealing with the death of my father. On this day I had taken the kids to school, and was rushing to an auction to find office supplies for my new office that I was preparing in my home. I had gone full-time into my company McKeithen & Associates Consulting in September. God was blessing me in this area, and I knew that this business was my calling.

My phone rang at 9:03 that morning. It was my friend Darnell. I was surprised because rarely did I hear from anyone in Cordele anymore. I had resolved myself to my life in Savannah, and was not looking back. So when the first thing Darnell asked me was, "Mona, you remember that baby you gave up? When was she born?" I was taken aback. I wondered why he would even care, but I told him "June 26, 1989." Then he said "was it a girl or boy." I was busy and didn't have time for games, so I said "Darnell, what do you want? You know it was a girl!" He interrupted and said, "Do you want to talk to her?" I still did not understanding the conversation. Then he said the words that caused my head to spend wildly, and my heart to race. He said, "Do you want to talk to her, she is on my other line."

Oh my God!! I had just looked at her picture one week earlier at Thanksgiving dinner, while talking with the kids. I looked at her picture, held back the tears, and in my heart I prayed that one day I would find her. I was still counting down the months, and had the search packet on my desk that Parent and Child Development Center had sent me two years prior.

I rambled many questions at Darnell within two minutes. He told me that he had received a text message from a strange person at about three in the morning. The text message said "I am trying to find my mother Mona Lisa Black." It hit him that this was the baby that I used to cry about, but he was scared that it may have been a scam also. That was why he had to check out her story for two hours before he even contacted me. I begged him to give her my number. I could not wait another moment. I had waited 20 years for her.

When she finally called, I heard the voice that my heart longed for, and it was pleasant. I found out that they had changed her name to Christina Nichole. That was a far cry from Vandy. Within the first couple of hours we talked about so much I was overwhelmed.

That entire day I felt as if I were in a fog. I had to call my children and tell them that Vandy had found us. I called my Aunt Barbra, who did a praise dance and shouted over the phone. Then I finally called my mother, and she cried as she begged me to tell Vandy to call her.

In all the talking that we did, I forgot to ask her what she looked like, so just as we were getting off the phone for the second time I requested a picture from her. When the picture came through, I was shocked to see that this young lady had my face, and was almost identical to Courtney.

For the next couple of weeks, there would be many times that I would cry. My children have called me "mom" over 3 zillion times since they were born, but something in me felt needed, wanted, and complete the day when Vandy texted me and said, "Thanks mom."

Exactly one month from the date that I heard her voice, she was standing in my living room hugging me, as she came for her first visit. Then she returned on May 6, 2010, and I spent my first Mother's Day with all of my children. My parenting life was made complete on that day.

I wish that I could say everyone was happy about Vandy finding me, but that would be a fairytale, and I told you from the beginning of this book that this was not that type of story. However, I thought that I would be able to tell the woman that raised her "*thank you*" soon after I spoke to Vandy. But her adoptive mother was not happy about her finding her birth family, and she remains that way. However, I have forgiven everyone that played a part in my 20 years of anguish, wondering what had become of my child. I pray that one day she will want to meet the person that gave her the wonderful gift of love, but until that day, I release the past and continue to work on my relationship with my daughter.

CHAPTER 7

The Final Deception

It was a normal holiday season for me. I was in Cordele not looking forward to Christmas 2007. My father had just passed away in September, I didn't have a job yet, and Dallas was still sick. I had moved in with Jackie and her family. After months of looking for a job, I had run out of money. Even though she chain smoked cigarettes, snorted coke, and had unseemly friends; then she brought her brother to live with us whom was a recovering crackhead who chained smoked also; it was better than living on the streets. However, I am allergic to smoke, so I spent long hours locked in my room with my children. So as Christmas approached I really didn't want to go to Savannah to see my dysfunctional family, but I needed to breathe some fresh air.

So I left for Savannah on Dec 23. I knew that my first stop would be going by my mom's house to drop the kids off. Then I would put on my street clothes and hit the club scene. I always started out at Sharon's Lounge because aside from having the strongest drinks, the owner was my friend Allen Scott, who I most times referred to as my brother. Allen would catch me up on all the street gossip and tell me who had died, gone to jail, or fought since the last time we talked. Usually after leaving him I would find my way to the area gay clubs so that I could decide if I were going to play with someone's' wife or daughter that night. I still tried hard to stay low key, so unless I knew the woman good, I was not going to mess around in Savannah too much.

So as I entered Sharon's all the neighborhood guys that referred to me as "Black Widow," not only for my pool shooting skills, but also because they said I could kill a mans hopes; they greeted me. I made my way to the bar and called out to Allen who came from behind the bar and hugged me. Allen could not talk long because the club was crowed and busy due to the holidays, so I made my way around to mingle. Just as I walked out the front door to catch some air I looked to my right and my eyes met with the eyes of a familiar face.

I could not remember the name, but I knew that face. As he walked towards me with those big brown eyes, pecan brown smooth skin, a little swagger in his walk, and a smile that lit up the lateness of the night, my whole body froze. I said "Hi", and he said "Hey", as if singing the word out to me. Then he asked how I was doing, like he really knew me. We stood at the corner of the street and talked for a while. Since it was already about one in the morning we both looked at each other and asked if breakfast would be possible.

As I stood there I noticed that there was something different about this man. Aside from the fact that he was the dressiest man in a "hole-in-the-wall" type bar, he was holding a bottle of strawberry flavored water. He told me he did not drink or smoke. I was intrigued by this, and the other thing that made him different was that he never once commented on the fact that I was fine as hell; like most men do. So already he had several points in the "yes" column.

By the time we sat down at breakfast this man had told me his whole life story. He told me that he was single. He said that he had been married once, but that was long ago. Then he told me that God had changed his life while he was doing prison time on a gun charge. He told me that he used to drink heavy, sell drugs, and was a coke head also, but God changed those things also. He told me that he had kids. I listen to every word. Then he said something that made the hair on the back of my neck raise and my ears burn. He said, "I am not looking for a girlfriend, I am looking for a wife."

After listening to his life story, I told him a little about me, but not all because I didn't want to scare him. However, I did tell him that I was an in the closet lesbian, that had never been in a "real" relationship. Because by this time I had come to terms with the fact that I only dated men out of necessity. Nothing about men attracted me, or made me love them. Then I told him that I had kids that I love and family down in Savannah that I was very comfortable not seeing more than once a year. He responded by saying "I don't feel that it is God's desire for you to be *that way*. You were made for a man."

I really enjoyed our conversation so much, until I didn't even realize that it was about four in the morning as we were preparing to leave. However, when Ricky said to me, "I want to take you out tomorrow," I agreed, and asked "Where are we going. That is when he said, "Church." My mind said, "What the?" We just left the club, and I had never been bold enough to do that before. Though I had heard that many "saints of God" do drink, party, and smoke on Friday and Saturday then show up for church on Sunday. Some even sing in the choir, preach, and usher. That was not my style. I kept a clear balance between my sinning and sainthood.

Now everything that this man had said to me in that two or three hours except for baby mamas and prison time, sounded like Greek to me. First of all, I had never heard a black man talk about wanting to be married, most men; especially black men are usually pressured into getting married. Then usually when I tell a man that I am a lesbian they respond by asking about what the sex is like, and then they ask if I do threesomes or would I let them watch. That is usually when the conversation takes an ugly turn, and I leave.

This man had me out at 4 in the morning on a Sunday and not asking me to come back to his place, but he said let me take you to church in a few hours. Even though I did go back to his house, because I did not want to go back to my moms house that time of the morning. To my shock he let me sleep in his bed and he did not touch me. Yep! That's what I said; he treated me like a lady.

Hours later we got in his car and went to church. On the way there he told me that he was not going to be able to sit with me, but I would understand why when we got there.

When we walked into New Greater Owens Temple I sat at the very back. I was scared to even be in there because I knew the life that I had been living, and in the recent years I had gotten worse. I watched Ricky as he put on these white gloves and went to the front of the church and stood right next to the pulpit, where the pastor and all the elders, and deacons sat. Ricky was the lead usher, and very proud of it. As I looked at him I had a good feeling about him. I really liked him, and he had already told me that he loved the Lord, and he was a man of God.

Services were really good. After being there for four hours we left and went back to his house. He told me that he had plans to be a deacon, then a preacher one day. I told him I just wanted to be a faithful member, because up to that point going to church more than once a month was hard for me.

My three day trip was turning out to be really nice. That was until I left church and went to my mother's house. Boy the devil must have known that even that day in church with my lesbian self, I actually wanted to change. But the devil will use demons to steal anything that you think you get from God. So that day the demon of choice was Marie Stewart with her fussing self.

Since daddy had died my mother did not have anyone to scream with all day, so she would catch her unsuspecting children and grand children when she wanted to fuss. On that day I was the target. Mom fussed at me so much that I went out to my car with a pillow and blanket then laid on the back seat. While in my car I called Ricky. On a night like that I would have either called Marcus, who was my hanging out partner when I visited Savannah, or I would go on the internet and find a woman to meet up with. Talking to Ricky during this time made me not want to do those things. He was saying all the things that I always wanted to hear a man say.

I found that we had many things in common. I still could not remember how I met him, but Ricky told me that we went out couple of times almost 18 years prior. This memory lost was common for me because by this time there were memories that I had that were so horrific that God protected me by not allowing me to remember segments of my life.

Ricky was a poet like me. He could sure put some words together, and even if it were all lies, he could convince you that it was the truth just by the way he spoke or wrote it. He made his life seem like things just happen for no reason to poor Ricky, and all he need was someone to partner with him and encourage his dreams. That's what he wanted me to believe.

Very often during our first conversations he would mention his children. He told me that he had six kids. Two were grown, and four were under the age of 15. He told me how much he loved his kids. That put about six more points in the "yes" column for him, because all I had ever encountered was sorry men that didn't take care of their kids (John, Edwin, etc...). He had three baby mamas, but I did not judge him for that. Heck, how could I?

By the 28th of December I had gone back over to Ricky's house again. We sat in the room and watched TV and talked all night. Oh my God, as I looked at him that night, something in me was starting to move. I had never had that feeling for a man while I was sober. Out of respect for him I would not drink during our times together. I knew he was a recovering alcoholic, so I didn't want to tempt him.

That night as I looked in his eyes that seemed like they were reading my soul thoughts, and I listened to his words that talked about how he was living for God and how at peace he was, he leaned over and kissed me. He kissed me like I was a gentle flower or a fragile piece of paper. That kiss caused me to extend my trip until Jan 1st. Lord this man was making a trip that was only supposed to last three days, last almost two weeks. After lying in his arms all day and all night with him never doing anything other than holding me, I felt like there was really a God, and he had given me a king. Finally!

The next day it rained and we only got up out the bed to brush our teeth and eat a little. I knew it was dangerous for us to be spending all this time in bed and alone, but that was the slow lullaby into deception.

I had no doubt that this man was a godly man, but he was laying in the bed with all these thick hips and thighs, and I must admit that I wanted to see if this feeling was real. So I climbed on him, and my spirit took over and every part of him gave in. For the first time I actually gave myself to a man without the assistance of alcohol or porn, and even though it was not the best sex I had ever had, it was the greatest because I wanted him.

It was after that night that all of my memories of Ricky came rushing back to me from when I was 19 years old. The reason why was because I had had sex with him back then. I remember it was awful! God had blessed him with good looks, but in some areas He had forsaken him greatly. He was not blessed in the male anatomy area. However, it was his talk that hooked me.

I went back to Cordele with a new feeling. All I could do is think of this man Ricky L. Williamson. He had definitely made me start thinking that a wonderful life could be out there waiting for me. Hope had sparked in my life.

By the beginning of January 2008 I had a new job in Macon. I was commuting 60 miles each way to work a state job that was paying me fifteen thousand less than what I was making before I lost my job at the hospital. But I didn't even care because I was working again, and looking forward to taking care of my kids. I had even moved out of the "smoke pit" (Jackie's House).

Things were even better than that because Ricky would call me everyday at 6 am. We would talk the whole time I was driving. I enjoyed talking to him about our future. I enjoyed him telling me that he felt I was smart and giving me advice when I asked. Then at night we would talk for hours, and right at 10 we would get off the phone, and he would follow that with a text message telling me how much I meant to him. Then if that were not enough, he wrote poems for me, which made me, feel so special.

It was a surprise to me that one day in February I said something as we were hanging up the phone that changed the direction of our relationship. As we said our daily morning good-byes he said, "Okay, go to work and have a good day." I said, "You too, I love you," then I hung up. In an instant I thought, oh my God, I said--*I love you*? He called me right back, and he said, "You slipped?" I said, "Yeah", but I didn't take it back. I did love this man. After that day he would frequently refer to me as free falling.

Okay I am going to slow down at this point because I have to show you something. Let's refer back to when this "man of God" told me that he was not looking for a girlfriend, he was looking for a wife. However, the subtle hints he was sending when I would tell him how I felt or when I would let the word "love" come out of my mouth was that he was not feeling what I was feeling. He called my feelings *free falling* because he was totally holding on to his emotions. Those were his words of warning. But that did not stop me.

For the next three months I was making a trip to Savannah at least three times a month. I had stopped drinking cold turkey. Ricky had become my drug of choice and I would do whatever I had to in order to get to him. He played a good game too. Every week he would ask me on Monday if I needed any money. I was not used to that. I was not used to a man trying to provide for me without treating me like crap. That was the reason why it was easy for me to think that God must have given this man to me.

By March I had come to the church so many times that many of the members knew that I belonged to Ricky. I enjoyed watching how he walked around the church and was a faithful usher. I felt good just to carry his bag at the end of service, and walk behind him. We looked so good together, and by all outward appearances we were the perfect couple. However, there was something that I didn't know about the church, but I found out the forth Sunday in March.

I often times wondered why Ricky always discouraged me from getting to know too many people in this church that he surely seemed to love. He would tell me that all the single women in the church wanted him, but he didn't have time for them because he wanted a classy woman. He told me that they were going to dislike me because I had him. That gave me a little ego boost to know I had the man every woman wanted.

But every time I would attend the church I would frequently see this very dark skin, shapely, pretty woman with a baby. I didn't know why my eyes would almost be fixated on her like I knew her, but that day as she sat holding this baby of not more than 5 months old, I saw Ricky go to her. He reached for the baby, but the look I saw in his eyes told me that this was no ordinary little member of the church, and the look she gave me told me that she was a baby mama, and I was that other woman (formally known as "That B")

My mind told me that there was some mess behind this, but I did not want to see it. Ricky had frequently talked negatively to me about all of his baby's mothers, but I would always stop him and say "Don't talk about her like that because if she is trifling now, then she was that way when you were with her. If she is nasty and don't clean up now, then she was like that then." I always kept in mind that if a man will talk about a woman to me, he will talk about me to the next woman. Remember that ladies.

So as we left church that day I asked him who the baby was, and he told me that was his baby. I did the math in my head and was sure that we were not together when he was conceived, but he was so young that he had to come in this world just as I was walking in the picture.

It concerned me that he would take me into a church that obviously he had history in, and not tell me that it might be a mess. That is why I felt the uncomfortable stares. I said to myself that day, that this man had left this woman while she was pregnant, and the church members were looking at me as if I were the reason.

He mentioned to me once how he told this woman that he didn't want anymore children because he already had five, and she had seven, but she got pregnant anyway. Well, in that conversation I told him that most grown people know what it takes to make a baby and it was not all her fault. So he never really brought that up again. However, in all of his talking, he never told me where she and the baby were.

In the back of my mind I felt uneasy, because I knew how it felt to be alone and pregnant. I was either left or just plain alone for all six of my pregnancies, and that was not a good feeling. That is why when she would look at me in church like I was trash or like she wished I would drop dead, I didn't even take it personal because I knew all that she was feeling. But finding out this man had taken me to the family church where his new baby and baby mama were should have told me that this "man of God" was messy and immature, but it didn't.

By now I was really in the deception game deep, but the devil was taking it slow. Ricky and I were going to church together on those Sundays when I would come in town, after we spent Friday and Saturday having all the sex that our bodies could take. He would get up and read the poems that he wrote to the church and I would support him because I was convinced that this man was Gods man. Even though right after we left church we would have sex, which was meant to hold me until the next weekend. Yep, we thought going to church was the pardon for all of our sins. Since I had never been dedicated to going to church I was just following him because by then I was tired of just being his girlfriend, I wanted to be his wife.

Back at home in Cordele I was battling all of my old demons. Many nights during the week I was having my girlfriend come over after the kids were asleep and I would get the fix for the lesbian that still lived in me. Even though I was in love with Ricky and enjoyed the emotional level our sex was on, I would still identify myself as a lesbian, and physically he did not meet my needs. Most times I would talk to him about the fact that I loved him but I was not attracted to men. However, I started telling him that I wanted to be free of that lesbian spirit. Going to church as often as we did caused me to believe that someday I could be free.

By March Ricky had planted a seed that would grow in me throughout our relationship. He told me one day that he usually does not date women as dark as me, or as heavy as me. So in the back of my mind, I wanted to make this man always feel that he made the right choice in allowing me to be a part of his life. My self-esteem was dipping.

Well, I think it was April or May when I found out that I was pregnant with Ricky's baby. On the same day that I found out I made my appointment at the abortion clinic, because I remembered his words of warning very clear, and the hurt that I would see in the eyes of his son's mother haunted me.

Let's stop right here for a moment. Ladies, the great poet Maya Angelou said ***"When someone shows you who they are, believe them; the first time."***

I could see that babies never held Ricky, in fact responsibility was the quickest way to make him flee (I would not learn that for another year or more). I didn't want anymore kids and baby daddy mess anyway. So I called him and told him what had happen and just what I was doing. All he told me was "I will give you half of your money back on Monday when I get paid." I told him when I would be going to have the procedure done, but he never told me that he would be there.

The day that I went to have the abortion there were women and their mates lined up in there, and mine was MIA (missing in action). He came by my daughter's house where I was recovering at later that day, but didn't stay long at all.

Now I know what you are thinking by now, and the answer is "NO". No, I did not see that this man was selfish and didn't know what real love was. I was still living off the fact that he wrote good poems, and was the president of the usher board.

By the time the abortion took place, I had already relocated to Savannah to work on loving him enough to be his good Christian wife. After that little brush with pregnancy and after the ten days he gave me to heal, he began doing something to me that made me feel so hurt, but I felt I had to accept it because it was what he liked.

Well the story is that in the first few months of our relationship I noticed that Ricky liked different types of sex than I was used to. I somewhat understood because when someone lacks in one area, they try to make it up in others. So if a man can't "hang" around long, he will try to make good for a woman orally. That is if he really cares for her satisfaction. Well, Ricky could stay for a good twenty minuets, and his oral game was nothing to fantasize about.

Then he had the condition of "falling short," that made him want to explore other means of enjoyment. Therefore, the first time he turned me on my stomach and sodomized me I prayed that it would soon be over. The pain and the nasty feeling that I had, was only soothed when he finished and would pull me close to him after we washed.

Most men that I knew did not enjoy that type of sex exclusively, so if I rejected them, it was not an issue. So when every time we engaged with each other he either tried, or insisted I began to wonder if his time in prison had anything to do with this desire.

I would often do other things so that we didn't have to do that, but I think his craving for that type of sex also came from the fact that he would spend countless hours looking at porn online. Yep, well by now I officially knew that my "man of God" was not who he showed our Apostle and the other members of the church.

However, Satan had allowed me to build this altar around my mind, and Ricky was placed up on it, and not God or Jesus could knock him down. I lived, slept, and breathed for Ricky. The ground he walked on was holy, if you asked me, and I was willing to cover all his sins by smiling for the public. However, I had begun to feel what my eyes could not allow me to see.

First of all I found that Ricky didn't respect me. I remember the first time I slightly allowed that feeling to filter through in my mind. Very frequently Ricky's baby's mamas would call him, so that did not bother me. However, one month after I moved to Savannah Ricky told me that the lady he was renting a room from had decided to move in with her boyfriend and sale her house. He said he was going to have to move. Well for about a month he rented a room from his cousin. However after going home several times and either not having water or not having A/C or electric, he decided to move. He didn't tell me and I had no idea that he was going to move in with Jackie, his twins mother.

Okay, I will pause to allow you time to say… "I know the Hell he didn't!!" Yes, he did!

August, September, October, and half of November went by and the man I loved was going home every night to his ex-girlfriend and two kids. Oh, and he didn't see anything wrong with this because he said, "If you really knew me, you would not even think that anything was going on with me and her." Well at that time I could not just call him a liar, that would be rude, cause it would be a while longer before I found out that he really was a liar, and in that situation, a bold face liar.

However, what I used was common sense! Ladies and gentlemen of the jury he wanted me to believe that he had obviously drew water from that well before, but being in the house everyday and night would not tempt him to drink from it again. Then when I told him how disrespectful I felt that was, he acted like I was the one with the trust issues. I told him that if we took a poll(survey) of 1000 women, worldly and saints of God, lets see how many would be cool with their mate moving in with his ex without even discussing it with her. Hell, with 97% of them it would not matter if he discussed it and wrote a twenty page paper on all the reasons why this is a good idea, the answer would have still been…no! Hell no! And for the down right worldly women…nigga you done lost your **bleeping** mind! You must think I'm a **bleeping** fool?! The other 3% would have killed him right on the spot and be staring on an episode of *Snapped* or *Deadly Women* right now.

Anyway, what further told me that something in the milk wasn't clean was the morning after he and I moved in together in November. We went to pick up his oldest son for church, which he had also moved over there to live with all of them. Yeah, they were one big happy family. Anyway, Jackie came down the steps looking really upset. She had tears in her eyes, and was shaking as she spoke to him. She was telling him that he needed to get all his stuff from her house. She was on the verge of acting a real fool. I could read in her face that she felt used and hurt, so that was really my answer to all the questions I had prior to that day. Then my gut was screaming and telling me that was a look of a woman who had sex with a man, recently.

However, I justified, and calmed the feelings that I was having by saying to myself…he is living with you now and not her. So I could have my family, because by this time that was all that I desired. Somehow I had fooled myself into thinking that marriage was going to keep me from ever wanting a woman again, that Ricky would stop texting other women in the middle of the night, and that his over eager desire for porn would go away.

So I cooked three meals a day, I cleaned, I made sure that I told him how handsome he was, and I encouraged him all the time. I looked pass the sex that was not satisfying. Then when that was not enough, I didn't just have one job, but I worked three jobs so that I could be a good help meet for my man. Oh, there was nothing too good for Ricky. I didn't have a car anymore because my engine locked up while Ricky was driving the car that I had moved down here with. Instead of me buying another car for myself, I gave him the down payment for a truck, and he would not even put my name on the title. Then he allowed me to use his old van. My friend Lisa told me that I was stupid as hell for that one, so you don't have to write me and say it.

I picked up my third job because I would frequently go into JC Penny and want to buy him things, but because I was paying most of the bills in the house, I rarely had extra money. By January or February they had increased his child support another $300 to include the last baby, so he was now paying over $1200 a month in child support. His checks every two weeks were about $600. So like a good wife to be, I felt it was my job to make sure the house did not go lacking. So one day I applied for a job at JC Penny just so I could buy clothes for him and the kids.

Ricky told me many times that he did not see me as his girlfriend, but his wife. In fact he told so many people that I was "the one", that I felt it was my duty to make sure that I was a good helper. Between my two primary jobs, the part-time one, and the contracts that I was getting through the business, I was earning very close to six figures a year.

I understood that he was not bringing home much money. By this time I was seeing that he was not financially responsible. I never knew when he was not going to pay a bill, or when he would not have his part of the rent. Because instead of talking to me and telling me that he was going to be short

I had to go to him the day that a bill was due to see if he had his part. Most times he would not. It didn't even bother him. I was becoming increasingly unhappy, but I prayed things would get better.

In May of 2009 I received the phone call that changed my mind on who I was a little. I desired to be a member of Alpha Kappa Alpha Sorority Inc. since I was 23 years old, and attending Savannah State University. So on the this mundane morning when my phone rang and it was the Basileus of Sigma Alpha Omega Chapter telling me that I had been selected to attend the intake process for this prestigious organization, I pulled my car over and cried. I was so happy. I had finally been accepted into something. I called Ricky immediately, and though he did not really understand why this meant so much because he had never been to college, he saw the potential for me being able to network and make more money to take care of him with. So, the day that I stood in front of about 400 people, read a poem that I had written and became a part of the history of Alpha Kappa Alpha Sorority Inc. was the proudest moment of my life. He was even proud of me, and that made me feel even better, because just like my father, I wanted Ricky's approval.

Living like the primary provider for a independent woman, who was convinced that the "man of God" was the person she was supposed to marry would not have been so bad if he was treating me like he loved me. I felt like I was lucky to have him, and he made me feel fat, ugly, and not worthy of love. I say that because he would drop subtle hints like, "you should lose a little weight." I was always a woman who dressed up, but I found myself putting on make-up and trying to get super sexy on the weekends, only to have him look at me like I was his mother. He always wanted me to comment on his appearance, but many days I could not even get a "you look nice". I had to wait until other men in the street told me. Oh, but that was the next phase of my self-esteem heading south for the winter, summer, spring, and fall. It seemed like the worse he acted the more I wanted to please him.

Throughout that time I did have one friend that was warning me to leave him. Lisa was the only woman that I had ever met that I really looked up to. She was strong, beautiful, a business woman, and opinionated. When I met her I could tell from the start that she had a spirit in her like me. Yep, she was a lesbian also, but that never mattered. However, Ricky was not happy with our friendship at all. I didn't know whether it was because she could see the things that I could not in him, or if he was scared that I would be tempted to resume my other life, which by this time I had not visited in over a year. By the time I moved to Savannah I had not even taken a phone call from any of my ex girlfriends, or women that I knew I could sneak off with. I can't say that

I did not think about being with a woman, especially since things were not going great with Ricky. However, in August 2009 I was tired of his mess.

By this time I had stopped going to church with him because I got tired of seeing him playing with God. The church had changed also, and even though I knew nothing about the mess; I could feel that the sweet spirit of the church had changed, and by then I really needed a move of God. I was in bondage!

I had been praying and reading the bible a lot by then. It was my only form of comfort because my primary job was not going well. Then my two part-time jobs were just draining my energy because they required me to work until ten or eleven at night, and since I was depressed I only had enough energy for the daytime. I was pouring into everyone, but I had no one at that time that was pouring into me. The situation with Ricky and I had even caused a distance to be placed between Lisa and I.

With all the praying I was doing, Ricky was getting worse and on August 2, he had begun to go out more. He was not a street runner, and throughout our relationship there were very few times that he would leave and not tell me what he was doing or where he was going. But this night he left, and did not come in the house until about 5 in the morning. I had been worried and upset all night, but I remembered from the last time that he did something similar, that I was not allowed to call him while he was out. He considered that act of my wanting respect, stepping out of my place.

When he came in the room all he said to me is "move over". Then when I did not move, he said it once more. That is when I took a bold act and said, "Where have you been?" He looked at me like he was saying in his mind "who do you think you are to ask me what I do?" Just the look hurt me to my heart. I did not know what I had done to deserve this type of abuse. Then when I held my position in the bed, he picked up the mattress and dumped me out of the bed. As I was falling to the floor and trying to grab hold to him to stop my fall, my "man of God" did something that I never thought he would do…he strangled me. He held his position on my neck until my body surrendered and dark was before me. Then I felt him slap me in the side of my head and punch me also. He then left me on the floor, fixed the bed into its former position, and laid down. He closed his eyes and went to sleep like nothing ever happen.

I was shocked, disappointed, and hurt that with all that I was doing for this man to make his life better, and encourage him, he would do this to me. So that day after he got up and went to church, I packed his things in his van and changed the locks.

Did you just think that you misread? Yes, I said he went to church after beating me. He took a shower, put on a suit, and went to play pretend at the church. If only his Apostle could see the Brother Ricky that I had grown to know she would have had the deacons tie him to the altar! And she would have been casting demons out until the next day.

Unfortunately, it was my responsibility to cast the demon out of my house, so I called my friend Zay to help me. When I told Zay what Ricky had done he came over to make sure that I was okay. Zay was in the house when Ricky came from church. Zay looked at Ricky like in his mind he was saying "Nigga what?" I think Ricky knew that look, so without a word he put what little items he could carry in his truck and got to stepping.

Ricky was too much of a punk to say anything to a real man. Though Zay was highly educated, and could hold conversation with the brightest of minds, he still had a lot of thug in him waiting to be released.

By the end of this day it was confirmed this man was not the man that I fell in love with, and my children respected as a father; but I still loved him and I wanted God to heal my Ricky and give him back to me. So by two weeks later he was coming over to the house again. We were actually loving towards each other and spending quiet time together. Things didn't feel so one-sided; Ricky was actually putting forth effort. I was still in love, but by this time God was pulling me also. God wanted me to submit to Him, and Ricky wanted me to continue in the relationship that was draining the life out of me.

By September all I was doing is praying. Ricky and I were going over to another church some Sundays, but the 2nd Sunday of September 2009 was a day I will never forget. I had felt like I needed to go to church, but Ricky said he was going to do some yard work that made him extra money, so he was not going that morning. I went to service feeling like something might happen, but not knowing what was actually going to happen. When I walked in the door Pastor Marsha Buford was up praising God.

I wanted to get into the service that day because I was just feeling down in my spirit. I began to worship God until I heard the Pastor call my name. I looked at her and she called me down front. She spoke into my ear and said, "The devil has been tormenting you at night about your past. God says that he is going to give you peace." Then she said, "Now God says that the demon that has plagued you for a long time is cast out NOW, and to return no more!" Then she laid her hand on my head and I dropped to the floor.

In that time between the peace I experienced and wondering how or why I was on the floor, I could hear the voice of God telling me that he had removed the spirit of lesbianism from my life. It was amazing! When I got off the floor I was walking to my seat when the Pastor came to me and put her hand on my stomach. I felt a jolt of something just as I took off and ran around the church. I felt I was running for my life, and when I finally came to myself I was sitting at the feet of Pastor Buford. I made it to my seat and

I heard this voice again that I knew was God, and then the strangest things began to happen.

First, I was thinking in my mind that I wished I had a piece of paper to write down what I was feeling, just as the thought was complete in my head this woman beside me leaned over and gave me a notebook. Then after I had this brand new notebook, I thought in my mind that I needed a pen, and before I could finish the thought once again, this woman that I didn't even know reached over and gave me a pen and two highlighters.

It was after this act of kindness that I began to wonder if I was actually talking out loud but I was too under the spirit to know that I was. However, my mind had begun to wish that I had a bible so that I could read a scripture that the voice was telling me I needed to read. And again, before I could finish the thought this woman leaned over and said "hey, you got a bible?" I looked at her like, "come on now, who are you and why are you reading my thoughts?" But I just looked at her with my eyes filled with tears because I knew at this moment it was God doing all of this. Then this woman that I did not know and had never seen before gave me a brand new, in the box bible. Now I am not talking about the $9.95 bibles that you can find at any Wal-Mart. No, this was a leather cover big bible that came in a box, like you find at the Christian book store.

As I sat back in my seat and looked at all these items I had thought of and received in a matter of minutes, I heard God again. He said "if you be obedient, as you think of it, I will give it to you." I kept hearing God say "obedience is better than sacrifice." I left church that day with a renewed spirit and a purpose.

Driving home I stopped to talk to Ricky, because I was so happy. I felt like much of the reason why we could never get married was because I was a lesbian and even up to that morning I always felt I might go back. So after I told him all that God had done and said, I told him how much I loved him and how there was nothing preventing me from giving my all to him. That was actually the only thing left. He sounded happy for me, but later that night when he came over I had to tell him that I really didn't feel good about having sex with him anymore because God told me to be obedient. He was not happy at that point, but he respected what I said.

A few days went by and things were going really good. Ricky was being really nice. We were talking in the middle of the day again and I was feeling like we had finally turned a corner in our relationship. I was happy traveling with him to my sorority meetings that were three hours away in Tifton Ga.

I had lost my job due to the company downsizing the day after I got delivered, but I was excited because God had already provided me with a contract that was going to pay me the same amount that my job was giving me. He was providing for me the way He promised. Then it was a blessing that I lost my job, because between the job stress and Ricky stress I had been in the hospital twice with my blood pressure 200/110 and having chest pains.

One night, after I cooked dinner, Ricky and I went to the room like we usually did. As I laid there looking in his eyes, and searching his face, he said to me "what do you want to do with me?" I did not respond, and looked confused. So he said "where are we going in this relationship?" That's when I told him "I love you and want a future with you." Then as if a choreographed dance, he moved towards me and kissed me so deeply and said the words that I had been waiting almost two years to hear, "marry me." I was overjoyed! Finally I felt that I had become good enough to be his wife. This was finally real for me.

We set the date for December 23, which would have been two years from the date that I met him. Ricky sent me a poem the next day that was titled "Soul Ties", and in this poem he called me his soul-mate. He declared his love to me. He even went to the church that I had been going to and told Pastor Buford that he desired to marry me. She asked him that day "Do you love her?" He responded by looking at her and said "I love her with all my heart." Then she asked him "Do you love God?" He boldly said "More than anything." This was the beginning of the plot for death that the devil was laying out for me.

During the same month that Ricky and I decided to marry, I was released by God to write this book. In addition, He also told me to finish the planning for Robin's House, which is a social service agency that will be for women and children that have been affected by domestic violence.

I was so excited, and I was deceived into believing that this excitement was going to last. I began to drink the word of God, and I was praying and talking to God the entire month of September and October. Ricky had finally received the gift of the Holy Spirit and it seemed that all was well. I was able to tell Lisa how wonderful life was again. However, do you know how quiet it is just before a war starts? Bombs were just about to start dropping in my life, and I would find that my spiritual fort was not strong enough to keep destruction away from me.

The showdown began one afternoon in November. By this time we only had one car for the family, because the engine had gone out on the van. I didn't have a job, but I had several contracts that was sending money into the house. This day began with me taking Ricky to work, then Dallas to school, then returning to the house to pray and do a little bit of work. I would have to start making my rounds again about 3 pm. And I knew that I had to be back near Ricky's job by the time he called me, or it would make for a bad evening if he had to wait. Ricky could leave anybody waiting for hours, but he did not like to wait for a second after he was off. I would find myself praying that he didn't call me before 4:15, because Dallas' school was 40 minutes from his job even on a light traffic day, and school was not out until 3:30 for him. So on this day I think Ricky needed to do something in town by 5. However, he never thought of me enough to treat me like I mattered as a partner, so he would never tell me what he was doing or where he was going when it came to business.

As my phone rang for the 5th time and it was him, I knew his Ricky Williamson attitude was going to flare up, so I did not answer. When he got in the truck he said, "man, didn't I tell you that I needed to be out of here by 4?" I said in my submissive voice, which was most times the tone I used with him, "I am only 15 minutes late." Then he said, "Nigga why you didn't answer your phone?" That is when I got upset, because I said to myself, what man would call the woman that he loves a nigga? Then I said, "Ricky, I am not going to be any more niggas in this car!" He responded by saying in the nastiest voice and tone I had ever heard him speak to me in "nigger (he added the "er" that time) you will be whatever I say you are!" Okay, the cat was out the bag, and Lisa was right, something was wrong with Ricky, and that was the voice of Satan using his mouth. Because Dallas was sitting between us watching our every move, I stop talking. The rest of our ten minute ride was filled with silent tension.

Our house was void of any conversation between us for two days. I was still cooking and cleaning, but I could hardly look at him. I thought that he would apologize when he saw how hurt I was, but just like the day many months before when he had brought his male cousin to live with us without even asking me; then one night when he saw me holding conversation with him in our living room, he took me in the room and called me a "trick"; He never apologized to me then either.

Ricky rarely ever would admit that he was wrong in any situation. Even after he had done something clearly wrong or something that he knew really hurt me, he would treat me very cold. He knew that I loved him so much that it wounded me on the days when he would see me and would not say a word to me. So usually by the third night he would pull me close to him and I would melt into his chest and would have sex just to bond back together. I would be sure never to bring up how I felt about what he did. I felt it was worth me putting my feelings on the back burner in order to keep the peace because I loved Ricky when he was happy. So what if I was not happy sometimes. I had my family there, and I grew up thinking that this was the way is was supposed to be.

We would always have pretty long days of good times after the bad time had passed. By November I started seeing the change in Ricky again. He had began finding these new friends. For the most part during our relationship Ricky never really went out for social things, or with many people. He would go to things at the church, and in the beginning we spent lots of time doing social things as a couple. When I was working my three jobs I used to take him out all the time. I took him to the movies, out to eat, on a murder mystery cruise, and we went to concerts and out of town pretty regular until I noticed that I was the one that was always responsible for paying when we went most places. But when money really got tight, we spent more time at home.

When he told me one day that he had made contact with one of his old friends name Kenny that was going to be helping him with his lawn care business, I didn't see a problem with that. In fact I felt it was good he had help because he could do more work and bring home more money. However, Ricky told me that back when he was snorting cocaine and drinking, Kenny was doing crack and drinking.

The issues began when Ricky told me one day that him and Kenny were going to play cards at our neighbor's house. I thought to myself that Ricky should not have anything in common with an unemployed crackhead, so why would he want to hang out with him in social settings.

That night as I was at the house and Ricky was across the street playing cards, I heard a knock at the door. As my daughter answered the door I heard a voice that I had not heard in over 19 years. It was a woman name Tracy C., and I was shocked for two reasons. The first, because she was actually at my door at one in the morning talking loud and looking drunk, telling me how I needed to come and support my man in his card playing. But the second reason I was shocked was because I never liked her messy black butt when we were in middle school and she was trying to date Edwin (my baby daddy). It turned out that she was married to the crackhead.

After I sent her on her way and Ricky finally came home at 2:30 in the morning, I told him that I didn't like her and wished that he would not keep company with them. I told him that a man that is supposed to be living for God should not be hanging out with those type of people. As a side note, I was leading by example because though I knew I had been delivered from lesbianism, I did not hang out with Lisa and her lesbian friends when they had parties and dinners at her house anymore, because I knew that was dangerous for me. However, he did not say anything to me that night, but by the mere fact that the following weekend and the next 14 weekends would find him with them and leaving me at home told me that he could care less about how I felt.

It was coming up on the weeks before we were to get married, and God kept telling me wait, wait, wait! I didn't know why, but I was very soon to find out.

At first I really didn't notice that Ricky was playing me for a fool. I know by now your thinking that there is no way that this man could have done all that he did up to that point, and a woman with a masters degree, running a company, and working on a PhD did not know this man was cheating. Well, I was blinded by low self-esteem, lack of confidence, depression, and heck...I wanted to get married.

I was still planning for my wedding which by this time had been pushed back because we had not done our counseling with the pastor, and because "Ricky said he could not afford to buy me a ring." I told him I didn't care, I just wanted to be with the man that I was in love with, and be right in the sight of God. So I was denying any feelings that was threatening my fairytale ending.

The days leading up to the end of the year were strange. I was upset because Ricky was going into the bible putting together words for this poem he titled "In His Image", but looking at him made me want to puke because he was anything and everything but Gods image. I didn't go to the church to listen to him deliver that poem because I was too scared that the entire building would catch fire. I don't really know what it means to grieve the Holy Spirit, but I was sure that Ricky was walking the line that night by standing up there boldly lying.

When the New Year began I had really bad feelings about where our relationship was headed. I am not going to lie and say that I didn't see the signs. God had been dealing with me by making me feel something in my spirit that was telling me that Ricky was not going to be my husband. But still my only desire was to be his wife.

I had begun to have dreams by this time that were sending me signs but tormenting me also. One night I had a dream that this figure that I could not see had shot me in the head. I bled very hard for a moment, but I did not die. The bullet went through my head and stopped in my throat. The hole in my head seemed to heal, but I could not tell anyone that I had been shot because I could no longer speak.

For many days after this dream I wondered what it meant. I told only Ricky about it because I thought he could help me pray about it. By the third day I asked God what it meant, and it was revealed to me that the devil was trying to take my mind because if he could take my mind he could shut me up. I prayed, rebuked the devil, and had Ricky to even pray for me (the devil praying against himself...that's funny). I thought God heard my prayers and He was going to block the hand of Satan for me. However, I had a date with destiny that I was not going to be able to cancel.

After the dream I had, Ricky continued to be out with the crackhead, Tracy, and others every weekend, but he started doing something different.

He began leaving the house for long periods of time in the middle of the week, late at night and others times which peaked my suspicions.

So one weekend in late January as Ricky was going out for the tenth weekend in a row, I got dressed and told him that I wanted to go. He looked at me like I had said something wrong. He told me that I could not go and that is what told me that something was really wrong. I pressed my feeling by getting in the truck, and for the next two hours as he treated me like the first 5 scenes of "Diary of a Mad Black Woman", I sat in my driveway with him telling me how stupid I was, and me begging him to stop treating me so badly. When I refused to get out the truck he drove me half clothed in the cold truck to the Waffle House took the keys and left me in the truck like a common dog.

I sat in the truck for 45 minutes very cold before I went into the restaurant and sat at his table. I had no make-up on; I had even come out the house with my hair pulled back in a pony-tale, so I was feeling so ashamed. He was trying and succeeding in embarrassing and hurting me. He didn't even ask me if I wanted to eat. After all the many times I fed his sorry butt! He sat in my face and finished his meal. As he was putting the last bite in his mouth, I got up and went to the car because I assumed we were leaving.

As I sat waiting, I realized that he was not exiting the building. He was making me wait and freeze in the truck only because he could. I felt helpless. I sat there reading all of these poems that he kept stashed in his black bag. I ran across the one that was titled "In His Image" and after I read it, I promptly ripped it into little pieces.

After another forty minutes of me sitting in the truck, he finally came outside. We returned to the house and I got out and went in. He was in the house long enough to send a text message to somebody, then he left. It was almost two in the morning when he left, and did not return until four.

I was in the bed crying bitterly. I kept searching myself because all I wanted was this man to know that I loved him and that I was willing to improve myself in any way just to make him happy. By this time I had decided that maybe he would really love me if I was able to get my PhD, so I started working on completing this degree. I had already started working on it before, but stopped when I met and fell in love with him.

Let's take a short break, because I know that you're saying some not so nice things right now. But just in case you're keeping score and *not judging*, by 2009 I had totally given up the person I was. I wasn't even thinking about being with a woman. I had just come off the best financial year of my life. I was cooking dinner every night and breaking during most days to cook and take Ricky lunch. I had fallen in love with all 4 of his kids living in Savannah, but I really treated his twins like they were mine. I would buy stacks of clothes and shoes for them, because Jackie just was not able. I wanted to please him so much that I had even started helping the twins mother Jackie out, because the more we helped the less she was pissed off, and the easier it was to get the kids on the weekends. I was paying most of the bills and 90% of the rent. All I wanted in return was for this man to love me and treat me like I was special. But I was getting far from that.

I had convinced myself that since Ricky was still talking a good game as far as loving the Lord, then he went to church every time the doors were open, maybe one day God would change his actions totally. Because it was not all day, everyday that he was this nasty mean, hateful, selfish person. Ricky was the sweetest, kindest, God fearing man you ever wanted to meet about four days a week, and as long as you did everything that he requested. Except for the night that he choked me, he had never laid his hands on me. However, I was beginning to realize that just because it was not physical, didn't mean it was not abuse. I had also been introduced to the word "narcissistic" and I was finding that his behavior was definitely a personality defect.

We had once again pushed back the wedding. In spite of the drastic changes that had occurred in Ricky's personality in the time leading up to Feb 13, I still wanted to be his wife, and keep my family intact. My kids had become used to him always being here, and Dallas loved the floor he walked on. I thought he loved them also.

Bookmark the previous paragraph, because you will discover the same thing that I did in a few moments.

February 11 started out like our normal days. I took Ricky to work, then Dallas, then resolved myself to my work for the day. Because our van had been broken for more than three months by then and Ricky was not making any moves to get it fixed, I decided that I would get a rental car for the rest of the week. I had set the money aside early because this was supposed to be our wedding weekend. But since we had once again not completed our spiritual counseling, I figured that we would just go on a romantic Valentines weekend, reconnect and plan our life in a less stress atmosphere.

I was very excited about that day, but something kept bothering me. Ricky told me the day before that he had a dream, and in the dream he said that a snake tried to bite him in his mouth. Even though it was not my dream, I knew after he told me that God usually spoke to me through dreams, and I really needed to know what his dream meant. I had no idea that by night fall I would find out.

That evening as Ricky lay in the bed; I kissed him and told him that I was going to boot-camp. By February I had decided that maybe I was too fat, because he had told me many times that I was bigger than he would like me to be. I also told him that after that the kids and I were going to stop at my mom's house. He told me that he would see me when I got back, and that he was so tired that he would be using that time to take a nap. So I left and had a very uneasy feeling as I drove into town.

Our boot-camp dismissed a half hour early and I ran over to moms house, but was gone within 30 minutes. When I got home I immediately noticed that Ricky was not there. I ushered the kids into the house, got back in the car and began to call Ricky's phone. It was no surprise that he didn't answer the phone, because lately every time he went out of the house, he would be out of reach. When he would come home he would have an excuse as to why all of my calls for hours would go unanswered. This night I felt a panic in my heart. I was determine to find out if it was my imagination, as he had told me several times recently when I questioned his honesty, or if the reality was that God was showing me what I already knew.

For twenty minutes I called him as I drove the highway to the crack heads' house. I was praying that his truck would be there because he was always telling me that he was there when he left the house for hours. However, it was no shock when he was not there, but I knocked on the door anyway.

When the door came open there stood Tracy, looking into my confused and hurting face. She took great pleasure in telling me that she did not know where Ricky was spending his time, but it was not at their house. Then she said something that cut me, she said "You need to understand when someone does not want you." That statement rang in my ears for several minutes as I drove down the street screaming, until my phone rang. It was Ricky, and all he wanted to know is why I went to his friends' home looking for him. I asked him many questions also, like where he was, and how long had he been making a fool of me. Then I heard the voice of a woman and as if this man never even knew me, he said "Hey, I'm gonna have to call you back." Then before I could say anything the phone went dead. I called and called, but he would not answer the phone.

As I returned to the home we shared I was distraught. My mind was racing as I heard a voice on the inside telling me to look at the phone records, that in two years I had never looked at, but always had access to. As I scanned the records one number that went all the way back to the beginning of January kept reveling itself. The voice on the inside of me told me that if I called it would be a woman on the line. As I dialed I prayed, but it was no surprise to hear her voice. All I asked her was "How long have you been dating my fiancé?" She said something very cold, but so true... "You should ask him." That answered every one of my questions, then I cried and told her how much pain I was in, but I heard his voice telling her to hang up the phone, so that is what she did.

The true meaning of his dream was revealed to me that night. Ricky's lies were about to confront him. I was hurting. I had been betrayed by the only man I had ever felt true love for. I had been betrayed by the person I thought was my friend.

I went to the store and brought the biggest bottle of liquor I could get. I drank half of it to see if it would dull the pain, but it didn't even come close to touching it. By two in the morning all I wanted Ricky to do is come home and lie to me. I wanted him to tell me that he loved me above all else, and he was sorry for the pain, but he never came home. I was left in the home we shared trying to calm myself, and this man was so cowardly that he could not even come home to face me.

That night I called his sister because I always knew her to be a kind person to me. She prayed for me right then, because my mind was betraying me due to the overwhelming hurt and pain. I wanted to die.

I sat dazed in the bedroom we shared replaying in my mind his last words, and the word of the other woman. My eyes scanned the room and they fixated on the closet full of his clothes. I thought of how he always wanted to be seen, and show off. As I looked at all of the purple, red, and other hot colored suits that he had shoes to match, which always made his look like an 80's pimp, or a country preacher. I figured out how I was going to hurt him.

Within two minutes I began taking all of the clothes, shoes, hats, ties, and ugly suits out to my rental car. I got in the car and just as I was pulling out of the driveway Tanny was pulling up at the house. I stopped the car, and she said "You okay girl?" I said in a broken voice, "Yeah, I'm fine." Then she asked, "Where are the kids?" I replied, "They are in the house sleeping." After I said that, I pulled off leaving her sitting there in her car.

As I drove, I devised my plan of action. I had already told myself that it would have been too easy to just take all of his things to the dump and throw them away. However, my goal was to embarrass this person that without regard made me the butt of his joke. So I went to Wal-Mart and picked up a gallon of oil and bleach. After I put these items in my car I drove three minutes down the street to Keen Transport, where this man had been pretending to be so high and mighty. I got out of the car under the cover of the night sky, and began emptying out the trunk of the car.

I stacked all of his clothes near the entrance of the gate. Then I poured the bleach and oil meticulously on each item. I wanted to leave this man that based his life on deception, with the same thing he left me with…nothing. Then I took one foot of every shoe that he owned and threw them near the sides of the gate. The other foot I took with me so that I could discard later. I scattered the clothes after the oil and bleach had time to work. Then I left, wishing that I could be there at 7:15 the next morning when the pain and lies that he destroyed my life with would affect him.

Yes, I lost it!!! I put down all the education, my submissive personality, and lady-likeness for at least 24-48 hours. All of the anger that I felt for him, and all that he had taken me through for the past six to twelve months was finally coming out, and I was anything but Godly.

By the time 72 hours had gone by the guilt had set into me. I was mortified that this man I that I loved so much; the man that I went to church with; the man I sought deliverance from my hidden demon for; the man I tried to treat like he was a king in spite of knowing that he had some flaws… had betrayed me. Then he made me act like a person that I was not. It had been years since I even desired to have a "Waiting to Exhale" moment. The last man that made me do that was Randy, and he totally deserved all of what I did to him.

After he found all of his clothes outside of the gate to his job, torn, or just plain destroyed, he went days without calling me, or answering the calls that I placed to him. At that point I just wanted some answers. I wanted the pain to go away. I wanted my since of normal to return to me. By February 17 it was far from easing. I was still trying to maintain my grades in school. I had fallen into a depression that would consume me for the next 72 days.

Well by February 18 Ricky began to call again. He had rightfully moved out, but he knew that I loved him, and that was the hold that he had on me. I know this sound stupid, but even though he had committed the highest offense against my heart, and me as the woman, then he lied in church and said he loved me; but I still loved this man. All I wanted was my family back, and with all his flaws, he was a major part of what I considered family. Even though I knew that God did not want me to have sex with this man, when he called me on the 19th I asked him to come to the house. This was a mistake, but it would be two months before I figured out just how big of a mistake.

When he walked through the door there I wanted my normal back, but I could not even look at him. I wanted him to hold me, because even though I was hurting so badly from what he had done, Satan had convinced me that Ricky was the only person that could stop my hurting. When he undressed and got into our bed I felt all the love that I had maintained through all of this. I had my back turned towards him. We had sat through dinner and him playing with the kids, but I never mentioned to him my hurt and disgust that I felt towards him. He rolled me over and kissed me like he had many times before and shortly there after he would lay on top of me. In that moment I felt hurt, but I still felt love. Then as he inserted himself into me, my emotions gave way to tears.

Though sex is not what I wanted, nor desired from Ricky that night, I needed him. I wanted him to tell me that he was sorry for breaking my heart, and sorry that I had to endure so much hurt and disappointment. I wanted him to tell me that he loved me. As he positioned me, pulled my hair and did all the things that he always did, he never once told me he loved me or that he was sorry.

Amongst all of the drama my life had suddenly fallen into, I had forgotten that it was almost time for me to attend my residency for my PhD program. I called my friend Lisa and asked her could she watch the kids while I went to my four day class. Well, she without hesitation told me no. It seemed that I was always finding people to call friends that I would give my life for if they asked me to, but most of them would think hard before they poured water on my burning body. This is how Lisa was. She was still very upset with me because she hated Ricky, and didn't understand why I loved him. So after she told me that she could not watch the kids, I considered the fact that I had already paid $1500 to take the class, so not going was not an option for me. I asked my daughter Danielle, and she informed me that she didn't have kids. Yep, I always tried to be there for her also, but since she became grown and entered into the lesbian lifestyle she took every opportunity not to help me also. My last option was the person that was originally supposed to take care of them before all of this mess occurred. Yes, Ricky.

Now up to this point I never had any reason to question if this man loved my kids. He played with Dallas a lot more than I did. He taught him how to do many things, and he was always concerned about Kay. Even with the older kids he treated them with respect, and helped them whenever they needed him. So I felt that even though we were separated, the kids would enjoy him being home with them those four days. When I called and asked him if he could watch the kids for me, he agreed to.

On the day that I left I had everything organized for him. All he had to do is be there with them, feed them, and keep them safe until I got back. I called him on Thursday night, didn't get an answer. I called the house and found that he had come and given the kids some food, but after waiting for him to return my call for hours I went to bed. The next afternoon during our break, my roommate RayShon saw me have a meltdown as I found out that Ricky had not spent the night with the kids, and my kids had spent all of Friday at home alone. I was too far into the four days to return home to Savannah. Danielle knew that the kids were home alone because Kay had called her, but she never went to check on them. When I returned home on Sunday afternoon my neighbors told me that they saw Ricky stop by the house three times during that entire weekend. I made a mental note that my assumption that he cared for my kids were wrong. What real man would leave an 11 and 4 year old children in the house alone for four days? When I finally had a chance to speak with him about this all he said was, "I had some things to do." In the back of my mind, I knew what he was doing. I let it go, just so that we could move past all of this. So now this obsession with this man had caused me to put my children in danger. Yeah, my mind was gone.

I had stopped talking about him cheating on me by March. We spent many days and nights together. I would prepare breakfast for him each morning whether he spent the night or not, then take lunch to him at noon, then dinner with the kids became normal for us. During my down time of not catering to him, I would spend hours crying or just sad watching America's Next Top Model. I looked forward to any calls that he would make to me, whether he was asking me to get up and make him breakfast, or asking me if I had money he could borrow. This had been our longest separation, and desperation set in.

I took no pleasure in anything, days would come and go, but the only days that I would feel a little okay was the three nights a week that Ricky would come over and have sex with me. I didn't even know it, but Ricky had turned me into a whore. I wasn't a prostitute, because he didn't leave money. I was just there to do every sick thing he could think of. I had been reduced to nothing. The worse thing was I had no emotional or spiritual power to stop this cycle of abuse this man was inflicting on me.

By April I felt that we were close to really getting back together. Our conversations had become lighter and less about what he had done. At that point I didn't really know if he still had that woman, or not. I assumed not, because he was spending lots of nights at my home. We talked at least three times a day, and even without me asking, he would come to the house usually hungry and with clothes that needed to be washed. I would without hesitation meet every need. Then we would resign to our bed, and after having sex, but feeling that he was only relieving himself in me, I would lay in his chest and wonder if a night would ever come again when I felt real peace with him.

By April 17th I was excited about the up coming weeks, because Ricky and I were born 25 days apart. I enjoyed planning parties or cookouts for his birthday, which was on April 21. The prior year I had a party at his job, took him out to lunch with all the balloons following me, and took him on a murder mystery cruise. He brought me a desk, and a card that said "*Thinking of you*", for my birthday. I usually never got what I wanted for my birthday and most holidays would go by with him giving me a verbal "IOU," but that was how things were.

I knew that we were not in the same house this year, but I made up my mind that I had to forgive him and move forward. This man actually had me believing that all was well with us. He even seemed concerned about me and my feelings.

The days leading up to Ricky's birthday were not as bad, because he and I were doing well. I was thinking that it would be real soon that we got back together under one roof. He was texting me daily asking me to send naked pictures, and sex flicks. I had fallen back into our pattern of doing things for him without thinking of myself. He had already spent the night two nights leading up to his birthday. Hey, things were normal.

Daily I was trying to shake my depression, but it was very hard. Up to this point I had cried everyday since February 11. Yeah, I was in a dark place. Kay would leave me crying in my room each morning, and when she would return in the afternoon she would find me in bed looking like I had been crying. Kay had all but taken over as Dallas' mother. If Ricky were not visiting, I spent all my other time in the bed, with the devil playing movies in my head of how I was nothing, and how I would never be loved. I could not pray, I could not read my word, and all my so call friends had stop calling.

When his birthday came, I had already told him that the kids and I were going to bake him a cake. He called me that evening, and said he was on his way. Well, hours went by, and it was about 11 at night when he finally arrived. I was upset, but I didn't say much. He treated me as if I had really done nothing. As he took off his clothes to get in the bed, he pulled me close and asked me "Are you upset with me?" I replied quietly "Yes," and resolved myself to just waking up in the morning feeling better. He left the next morning after breakfast. We had several conversations that day, but due to my disappointment from the night before, I kept our interaction that day short and sweet. I really wanted to go off on him, but all I could think of is that I was close to having my family back again, and didn't want to ruin it.

My mother called me at 5:20 in the morning on April 24. Her blood sugar had once again dropped, and she was confused, and not knowing what to do. I told her that I was on my way, and I ran out the house. I called 911 as I was entering the car, because in the 40 minutes it was going to take me to get to her, she could have fallen into the coma that I always feared for her. I called the two aunts that lived closest to her, and then I called Ricky. I asked him to go to the house and feed the kids for me, and to bring my school books so I could get my assignments done while I was waiting at the hospital. He agreed and told me that he would meet me with them. Well, when I saw him he looked normal. He said that he was going to get his haircut, and I gave him my two breakfast sandwiches that suddenly I didn't have an appetite for. As he ate them, he told me that he was going to see me later. Even though I texted him and called later that day, I didn't hear from him anymore that day. Because of our recent pattern, I knew this silence had a meaning behind it.

I have had six children, and it is my experience that by the end of the 8th month I become very uncomfortable. That lets me know that my body is getting ready for a delivery. I have had only one child the natural way, but I can remember that the morning just before labor was coming I would feel differently. I would not be in pain, but I just felt like something was going to happen. Well that is how I felt on April 25, the morning my life began transition. I woke up crying that Sunday morning. By this time I had been depressed for 76 days, so crying was nothing new. However, usually the crying started after I spoke with Ricky in the morning, or when he would come to the house and leave me. But this day was different.

Though I had been crying for about an hour before I even got up out of bed, I felt that I needed to go to church. I could not even try to be cute that day. Usually I would hide my hurt by dressing up. My whole life I would dress over my pain. But today, I didn't have the strength. I put on one of my AKA tee-shirts, a worn looking pair of jeans, and some pink and green Polo sneakers that had a little dirt on the top from my last walk in the park. I didn't put makeup on, and I could not even give myself the boost speech that I had been doing for more than a year ("Pull it together girl, and smile").

I walked in New Greater and sat on my usual seat, the last pew, waiting for service to start. I had cried my entire ride to the church, but I had no idea why. As I sat there the devil told me to get up and leave. I got up, and as I shot pass Paul, who was the usher at the door, he asked, "Mona where are you going? Don't leave." I replied, holding back tears, "I am not supposed to be here."

I turned to head to my car, and that is when Janice pulled my arm and said "Don't leave. That is what the devil wants you to do." I could hardly see her, because my mind was telling me, just leave. Then Paula the Prophetess came to me. She looked in my hurting eyes, and said, "I don't know what you are going through, but God has something for you." She took me in the bathroom, and continued to talk to me, and told me to sit up front. I sat near Tanny, Ricky's sister. She saw the tears falling from my eyes, and they were only getting worse as the time went on. Then she hugged me and said "Mona, I am so sorry, I didn't find out until yesterday either." My mind stopped. My heart stopped. What was she talking about, is all I wondered. But the voice on the inside kept saying something that I could not wrap my mind around. The voice was telling me that Ricky was getting married.

As I left the church that day, I was more confused and hurt than ever. I could not wait to get to the car. The first thing that I did was text Ricky. The text simply said "Please tell me that what I just heard is not true."

He called me back within five minutes. I searched his voice, but there was no hint to what this snake had devised for me. I asked him, "Ricky are you getting married?" The phone was quiet.

Ricky had **gotten** married on that Saturday.

Yes. The man I had giving my life over to for nearly three years, had turned up his nastiness. He had looked in my face, he had slept with me, had sex with me up to two days before he married the woman that he had just met in January, cheated on me with, and broken my heart for. A mere 71 days after he bust my heart open, he did the one thing I wanted more than life itself…He got married.

CHAPTER 8
Your Gonna Laugh

O kay, I felt you needed a little break. The last chapter was too much. But this is the continuation.

I laid in my bed feeling like a gutted fish. Ricky could not have inflicted more pain on me if he had taken a dull knife and inserted it into my chest and dragged it all the way down my stomach, and then poured alcohol in the wound. I found out that day that heartache is not actually in your heart if you love someone; it is in a deep place that nothing can touch. I cried in anguish, bitterly on my bathroom floor the next morning. I saw Kay as she looked at me wondering if this was the last time she was going to see her mother. She ran out the house crying that morning, and would have to carry the last sight of her mother screaming on the floor all day.

The phone rang about five minutes after she left the house and it was the snake. I begged him to tell me what I had done so badly to deserve to be treated so bad. The only thing that he said was "If I hurt you, I'm sorry." Yes! He said…IF I hurt you. This nigger (again Mr. Sharpton, there is no other word for this situation), had the nerve to say "If". Then the cold way that you see it on this paper, is the cold way that he said it. Now I know some trashy, nasty, dirty, atrocious, filthy men, but Ricky took all these words to a new level. We may have to contact Webster and request they add a new deeper word for this man. However, narcissistic, social predator are the only terms that adequately describes this scum of the earth right now.

I put Dallas in the car that Monday morning. I was still crying. I could not see. I literally could not focus my eyes. The devil kept telling me that I needed to run my rental car into a tree. He was trying to kill me and Dallas. I was floating between sanity and insanity. I had not slept for more than two hours in a night for more than 77 days by this time. I was slipping fast, but between my drifts with sanity I called Tanny. I told her the whole ugly story about how her brother was still coming to my house and making me think that he still felt something for me. He had been using me right up to the day he got married. He was making this woman think that he was a "man of God", but coming to my house and making me feel like a whore. That was the reason why he could spend nights at my house. That's why he could eat with us most nights. And the devil was revealing all of this to me, and all I could hear is laughter. Ricky was laughing at me. Tanny knew I had lost it, when I told her that I wanted death. All she could do is pray.

I drove around Savannah not knowing what I should have been doing, or where I was going. I didn't even realize that I had forgotten to take my child to school. I was a mess. I felt the pain in my soul was too great for me to make it out of this. Then sanity set in again, and I called Apostle Jefferson. I told her the story of how I was deceived by Ricky. I knew she was shocked, because I didn't know it at the time, but this man had gone to her and told her about him getting married. I kept telling her how tired I was. I told her that the devil was trying to kill me. Then she asked me where I was. I didn't even know so I couldn't tell her. But she kept talking to me. She kept telling me to hold on. At some point I found my sight enough to determine that I was on the highway that would take me to her house. It had to be God, because highway 21 was far from Hodgeson Memorial, where my son's school was. In fact I never even had to cross that highway to get to his school.

By the time I got to her house I realized that Dallas was in the backseat. As we entered into the mansion that my Apostle lives in, I hugged her, and then I fell on her couch. As if I were two years old, I balled up on her sofa and cried bitterly.

She rubbed my back trying to sooth me, then she did what Apostles do… she prayed. "Father I stretch my hand to thee, no other help we know, if you withdraw yourself from us, where forth shall we go." It was that prayer that caused me to calm. Then she sat at my feet and began to read from the book of Psalms. Psalms is the best book of the bible when you are in a dark place. The Psalms God gave me that day was 91.

I had to pull myself together for a meeting that I had to attend by noon. I know that I looked a mess as I left Apostles' house, but before I left she made me promise that I was going to come to tarry service the next day. I made the promise, but I was planning on being dead before that. I figured that if I were dead she could not hold me to the broken promise. The rest of the day I spent devising the plan.

I had attempted suicide many times in my life, but obviously I was not succeeding. However, I was determine this time was going to be different. I didn't want any chance of someone coming to find me, or stopping me. So when Tuesday, the 78th day came, I planned on taking Dallas to school, and going to a hotel with all the pills that I had collected in the past 3 months. I could find no reason worth living, except for the fact that I had children. However, my youngest children were watching the failure that I had become, and my older children had seen this all before, so they could care less. I felt I would be worth more to them dead than alive.

I talked to my friend Janet. She is a minister, and lives a whole half a state away, but anytime I needed someone to pray for me, or just talk she was there. I had called her the day before, but she was just returning the call that morning. I told her of the hurt, deception, and how stupid I was feeling. She gave me words of encouragement, and prayed for me. After we got off the phone, I pulled my car over to the curb, and I screamed out to God. "Lord why are you allowing me to hurt so badly?! And why won't you help me?" I was mad. How could He have let this snake hurt me this way?

That phone call with Janet brought me a few hours more. Even in my insanity I just could not commit suicide after a soul felt prayer had gone up. I also felt that because Janet was a new pastor I could shatter her faith if she prayed for me and then I committed suicide. So I went home and got in the bed with my tears. By 3 in the afternoon my friend Ron called and told me to get up and pick up Dallas. I couldn't tell him that I was supposed to be dead by now, so I got up. When I returned to the house I got back in bed for an hour. I got up and thought that I need to get a drink. I went to the neighborhood bar and ordered a double shot. I wanted to really get too drunk to remember that I had been made a fool of.

As I sat at the bar thinking about the fact that I didn't have a car of my own; I had not worked in months because of the depression; I had stopped writing my book; I stopped working on Robin's House; and the man that I bought a truck for was driving his new wife in it. On top of that all my so call friends had stop calling; and my past had started calling again, because I was getting texts and calls from women that I had been intimate with in my past. This made me question if I had really been totally delivered from lesbianism. I knew my life was messed up! The devil was reminding me that I never had this type of pain when I was with women. I was listening too. I thought that Ricky was somehow attached to my deliverance from lesbianism, and without him I was as good as back in the lifestyle.

That drink had no effect on the pain, but I was tired of the kids seeing me in this constant state of depression. So I didn't return to the house. After I left the bar I went to my friend Eileen's house. I got on her couch and cried for about an hour. Then I heard the voice of God saying "Get to safety". Right after that I remembered the promise I made my Apostle Jefferson, so I got up and drove to the church.

I had made up my mind that if I left that church the same way that I had done for two and a half years that they would be preaching my funeral by the weekend. I scanned the room for my Apostle Jefferson, but she was not there. As they called us to come around the altar, I walked up to Prophetess Paula and told her "I don't need the Holy Spirit, I need deliverance." She told me if that was what I wanted, then God would give it to me.

I had only come to the tarry service about 4 times since I had been attending the church, because Ricky always told me that he couldn't get anything out of it, and that he felt it was fake. I usually didn't get anything out of it either. Maybe it was the company I was keeping that was hindering me?

Well I got on the floor and began to call on Jesus. In tarry service the only word you have to know is Jesus, cause after you call *that name* a couple thousand times something is going to happen! Now trust me, I was not just saying a passive, "Jesus, Jesus, Jesus." I was saying Jesus! Jesus! Jesus! like someone was shooting at me. I was saying "Jesus, Jesus, Jesus" like it was going to be my last words. I was saying "Jesus, Jesus, Jesus" like He was the only person that could rescue me. But in the middle of my "Jesus, Jesus, Jesus," I could hear the devil telling me that I was so filthy and dirty that God would never touch me again. I got tired, but I still continued to call His name.

They have special women who they call altar workers that encourage you to keep pushing. Almost like a nurse when you're having a baby. So I would lose my strength and they would help me to get my desire back. I don't know how long my Jesus calling had gone on, but I could hear the voice on the inside of me saying "You are at the door. Come in." Then I heard the devil say, "If you don't shut up, I am going to kill you right here, right now!" He was mad. In that instant I felt sharp pains in my head like someone was stabbing me, and all the bones from my neck to the middle of my back and down my arms begin to constrict. He was trying to scare me into feeling like he had the power to kill me. Yeah, he put a hit on me right in the church! But I thought "I would rather die and fall into Jesus, than to let you kill me when I leave here."

At that point I said a JESUS like I had been stabbed in the back. I said a JESUS for my life! And something so amazing happened...I crossed over into laughter. I could not stop laughing. I laughed for what seemed like a few minutes before the voice that had always spoken softly in me, began to speak loudly out of my belly.

The first things that I remember God saying was:

"I snatched you from the hand of Satan!"

"You ARE who I say you are."

"YOU are a virtuous woman."

"I know the thoughts that I have concerning you, thoughts of peace, joy and love."

"My kindness will always rest on you"

"Living water will flow from your belly."

"Jubilee!"

"I'm giving it all back."

"My word will not come back void, and every promise I made you will see."

Then He told me "Look at the doors behind you," and I could see them. He said, "I closed them, but you keep trying to go back through them, so now I am going to remove the doors so you can't even find them!" Then He told me, "Look at the doors that are before you" and again I could see the doors, "I prepared them for you, and these are easy doors."

Then God said,

"The shame of your past is no more!"

"I can pull water out of mud."

"Long life I will satisfy you with. You will not die but live!"

"No more will you blend into the background, I am moving your seat to the front."

Then He said, "Tonight when you rest, you will be in my arms and know that nobody can love you like I do."

"You shall walk with your eyes closed, knowing that I will never let you fall." I asked right then, "Lord, how can I walk with my eyes closed?" He said, "By faith."

"You're going to write again."

Then God said, "If you knew where I was about to take you, you would laugh." And I laughed! And I laughed! And I laughed! I'm still laughing.

Oh, and I looked for the pain that Ricky had left in my soul, and it was gone. It was gone as if it had never been there, as if I never knew a Ricky Leon Williamson.

I don't even know how I made it home that night because I was laughing so hard. I picked up the phone to call my Auntie Barbra who I know had been praying for me. I excitedly told her all that God had done for me that night.

Then she told me something so amazing that I know it had to be God. She said "Lisa, God said that he had to allow you to go down to the breath of death, because this testimony will deliver many hurting women." I knew that was God, because she was not in my car earlier that day when I screamed out to God that question of WHY.

I laughed all the way in the house. I laughed in the shower. I laid down in the bed still laughing. I wrote my first poem, in more than a year since.

God gave me the title, "Healing in the Hurt". Then God settled my spirit and allowed me to sleep. I had not slept a complete night in 78 days.

I woke up one hour before I was scheduled to, feeling like I had been sleeping for 7 days. I smiled as I greeted God that morning. The sun looked brighter that morning. Then I got up. As I walked pass the mirror I turned and did something that I never liked doing. I looked at myself.

Oh, my God! I discovered something that day. I am actually a very pretty lady. You see, ever since the man raped me and left me for dead, I always looked in the mirror and saw a monster. I saw someone tar black with a distorted face when I looked in the mirror. That was the source of my low self esteem. But that morning in my nakedness in front of God I found I am not fat. With no make-up on, or even a wig, I was absolutely beautiful. It was as if I had met **ME** for the first time. I stood there for another five minutes, just smiling.

The phone rang at 7:02 that morning. I looked at the caller-id and it was the "devil" calling. I asked God "Should I answer this?" God said "Yes". See the devil had gotten used to hearing my broken, desperate, hurting voice each morning. So he was calling just to make sure things were still the same. He loved it. But when I answered the phone I didn't say anything for a second. The devil said "Mona, you up?" And as if singing a song I said "Yes, I am up! And let me tell you what God did…" I told Ricky the entire story within 5 minutes, all I heard him say in a dry voice was "That's good". Then I did something that most people could have never done. I said, "Oh Ricky, I just want you to know that I forgive you for all the hurt, pain, and anguish that you have caused me, and I pray God's mercy on your soul." Okay, that freaked him out. But I meant every word. I hung up my phone, and began my process of healing.

Okay, I know that you're thinking that this has got to be the end. Well, if this was an ordinary person it would be, but God made me special, so read on.

The following Sunday I walked with boldness right to the front pews of the church. I had never passed the first three from the back the entire time I had been attending that church, or any other church for that matter. This was because the devil had always held me in bondage, telling me that I was not good enough to go up front where the "saints" sit.

This was the same church that Satan told me I would never be able to walk in again without people laughing at me. I sat in the second pew with no shame or guilt. My Apostle got up and announced that someone in the church wanted to give a testimony, and she opened the floor for the lady to come. After that sister talked about helping, and her health, a blind man got up and sang a song that was so beautiful I began to cry. It was titled "Walk with me Lord".

Then, as if something was burning in me, my Apostle looked at me, and invited me to the podium. I walked boldly up there to the front of the church and said, "Everybody has a story, and here is mine..." The Holy Spirit took over, and I told the entire church about me being a lesbian, how that snake Brother Ricky mentally and physically abused me for two years, and in the end almost caused my death. I don't remember everything that was said, but I remember running free and I started dancing! I was free y'all!

I was sweating from dancing so much in the sanctuary, so I went to the bathroom and not knowing all that I had said or done, Tanny came and got me. She said "Mona, look what you did!" Then she opened the door to the sanctuary and I saw people celebrating, praising God, getting delivered, and hugging each other. Then God said, "This is only the beginning." As I walked into the sanctuary, Ricky's nephew gave me a big hug and told me that I inspired him. Wow!

Bonus Footage

Well God gave me revelation for a few things that I have to share with you.

First, He told me that you HAVE to forgive. I want you to forgive everyone and everything from your past, because it will hold you in bondage.

Between the time of the old season and the new season, we come to a point of decision. The place of decision is what most would call the valley of life. This is the place where you can review the past, and finding nothing to go back to is the point where knowing that what is to come is better than where we have come from.

When I think on all the promises that God has made to me about my life, He told me that my book will be number one in three years. He called me a woman of virtue. He said that He would give me the desires of my heart. So I had to realize that my season is about to change. I had to review my past and where I was. The things that I saw were not good. However, I had the promises of God which gave me confidence that my latter would be greater than my former.

I was a woman who questioned her sexuality. I was living in poverty despite my education and training because I lacked confidence in who I am, and the gifts that I held on the inside. My self-esteem made me feel ugly and I always seemed to meet people that would feed those feelings of insecurity and made me feel unworthy of real love or friendship. I was interacting with men and women on an unhealthy level, always trying to give them more than I expected from them, and then feeling used when they only did what I allowed them to do to me.

Maya Angelou said, **"A woman's heart should be so well hidden that a man would have to seek God in order to find it."** That night that I got delivered, God told me that He was going to hide my heart in Him, so that I can never be deceived again.

In my past I exposed that I was hurting, confused, lacked self worth, and was searching for love, and because the devil had a plan to destroy me since I was a child, he would send men that would rape me emotionally so that I would never heal.

However now in my place of decision I realize that my destiny is not locked in my past, it is secured in my future! So I can let go of my past.

Now this is for all of the people that question who they are. Don't be deceived. The devil will tell you that the feelings that you are having for the same sex is normal because you were born that way, but he is a liar. These types of spirits enter into the generational blood line just like the gene that causes cancer, diabetes, or high blood pressure. This is called a generational curse. Yes, it may be in your blood line but it takes something to trigger it to wake up in you.

I look around my family, and I realize that this issue of lesbianism is not just my issue, but I have a few cousins and now a precious daughter that are struggling with it. Not to mention the down-low men in my family. The trigger that woke this spirit up in my life was sexual perversions that happen to me at a young age; me watching porn from the age of 12-39; not having high self-esteem; being used and abused by men; and letting others tell me who I was and speaking negativity over my life.

If you have ever questioned your identity I am sure you can identify with one of the issues that I pointed out. But my sister and my brother, don't be deceived, God made women to love men, and men to love women, in a healthy way. But the devil will send people that will encourage any issue you have.

You were not born an alcoholic, a whore-monger, a lesbian, a homosexual, or any other thing that has positioned itself as a stronghold in your life. You were Perfectly and WONDERFULLY made by God.

Oh and let me take this time to tell you something special that God showed me. He told me that the fact that my cousin was chosen as a vessel by Satan when I was 4 years old to touch and molest me, that turned on the spirit of helplessness. Then when the white man kidnapped, raped, and left me for dead, that turned on the spirit of fear and feeling differently from others. Then when my father told me that I deserved what that man did, that turned on the spirit of ugliness, unworthiness, inferiority. Then, when I would go into my brother's stack of porn magazines and became comforted by the visions of women, this opened up the doorway to lesbianism. Then as I grew, all of these spirits were fed by others.

But God said it was not about my childhood, He said it was about Satan stealing God's plan for my life. He said it was about keeping me out of where God had planned for me to be. It was about distracting me so that I would lose sight of who I am. It was about killing my spirit before God had the chance to bring me to greatness. God had to be the one to tell me that it was the devils plan to cause me to lose my mind before I could finish the writing of this book. God had already told me many years ago that He was going to make my name great, but the devil tried hard to steal that thought out of my head.

However, God will set up in the spirit all the things that will take place in the natural. He had already set up the spirits that would be warring for me against the devil when the stakes were increased. The devil said, "Okay on April 24, 2010 I am gonna take her out, never to return again, because I will use what she loves the most against her. I can't kill her, but I am going to make her kill herself."

But God said, "NOT SO"! Then He knew I had been beaten down for 78 days, and could not fight anymore. So, He caused Tanny to pray. He caused Apostle Jefferson to pray. Then he caused my Auntie Barbara to lay on her face praying and warring for my soul. Then he caused Pastor Buford to grab hold and tear down some strongholds in my spirit. Then He sent his voice calling me, causing me to reach deep down and make connections with the only help I know, Jesus! And that is when true and complete deliverance and healing took place.

Soon after my deliverance, the fiery darts began to fly. The first one came one week after Ricky had gotten married. He called me and asked me if he could borrow $300. The devil is bold. I took great pride in telling him, "You need to ask your wife." Then he said that "I thought that we could be friends." And I told him "I would not want a friend that would treat me the way you have done…get real!" But the devil has no shame! I am telling you! The next week he called me and said, "You need to leave the church, because me and Destiny (the wife) are going to be coming back." He taunted me about me not being ordained to be his wife, and even questioned my intent for wanting to still attend the church that I had been at for the past 2 ½ years.

Now the devil had just made me angry. So I told him, "Does your wife know that for more than two months you lied to her? Does she know your character, or that you lack morals? If you bring her to the church your wife will be the only one in the church that does not know you deceived her right up to the altar. Did you tell her that you owe over $50,000 in back child support? You're messy and I thank God that I am not her. I can walk with my head up high because I know who I am, and who I belong to." Then I asked him, "How are YOU walking?" Then he hung up.

See, you have to talk to your devils and not be moved, and then they will flee!!

About eight weeks after they got married, we had our pastors' anniversary celebration. For the first time I had been asked to be on the program. I was honored to speak on behalf of the woman that was partly responsible for saving my life. So that night I walked into the church dressed as if I was First Lady Michelle Obama, with the swagger of the President. I immediately saw Ricky. After all he had done, and the fact that he had not been in our church for at least four months, he had the nerve to be standing as an usher at the door.

I didn't let his presence break my stride though. I smiled and kept moving. Then, during offering, as he and his new wife approached, she "mean mugged" me. This homely, misshapen woman was looking at me as if she had won a prize, or done something that I was not able to do. Well, instead of turning up my nose, or lowering myself to their levels, I smiled so prettily at her that she stumbled. In fact, I laughed!

I was laughing because the word of God says, "That which a man sows, he shall surely reap." Then I lifted up my hands and thanked God that I was free, and I asked Him to have mercy on her because she is about to meet the man that I already knew. Ricky had not changed, he just changed partners. She would soon be in the same bondage.

Ricky and his wife were able to witness how God was beginning to use me in ministry, because my welcome address to the church was awesome. After that night Ricky never returned to the church.

Then for weeks and months after that, different people tried to relay to me all of the negative things that Ricky was saying. However, I was not moved at all. I distanced myself from everything connected to him, but I still continued to love his children and provide for them when I could.

It was finally very freeing to see myself the way God sees me, instead of being defined by others. It was good to be able to finally let go of the past, and know without a shadow of a doubt that God is the author of my book of life. It was good for me to know that I could never fall off the floor, because the floor was the lowest that I could ever go without the ground opening up and taking me. But in being on the floor, I found that there was nothing else to do but get up.

So I command you that if you feel you are on the floor, GET UP! And keep getting up! It has been less than one month since I was delivered, and I have true JOY!

The end..."NO" The beginning!"

78 days… "7" the number of completion, and "8" the number of new beginnings! Praise God!

AND LAUGH!!!

Reflections

As I look back over the last forty years of my life, I realize that though my life has not always been great, I have accomplished much more than some people had done without all of the obstacles that I have. I found out that I am very intelligent, kind, wise beyond my years, and beautiful!

I allowed my past mistakes and abuse to hold me back from where God had already planned for me to be before He even made me. I allowed other people to define me, and tell me how my life should, or could be. I never took the time to find out who I really am.

The night that I was delivered was a very significant day. April 27th was the birth date of my natural father, who because of his illness, and nurturing, was unable to show me the love that I rightfully deserved. But on that night God became my father replacing my natural one. Then God showed me something when He spoke and said, "I can pull water out of mud." You see, up to that point my life had been so muddy, murky, and dirty that I never could see any good coming from it. Water is pure, and it gives life. He was telling me that out of the life that was so horrific, disappointing, and at times seemingly not worth living, He was going to make something so good from it that people would never be able to look at me the same way again. That is what it means in the Bible when it says that He works all things for the good of them who love him and are called.

After the scales were pulled from my eyes, I realized that I am a mother, sister, teacher, friend, well-educated, successful business owner…and the list goes on, but now to add to that list, I am an author, and motivational speaker. Wow! Imagine that!

I also have reflected on the people that I hurt while I was out there hurting. I acknowledge now that I have broken up some marriages, lied to people, lead some people astray, and never looked back. I have gone to many of them in the recent months that I have been writing this book to ask for forgiveness, and I have gone to God. However, I will never be able to locate them all, but I pray that this book will find its way to each of them, so that they will know that I am truly sorry.

I thank each one of you for coming with me into my journey. I hope that my story of redemption will allow you to close the doors of your past, and move forward in the love that God wants to give you freely.

Special Thanks to:

All my haters! To the people that used me, disappointed me, abused me, hurt me, lied to me, talked about me, and anything else you may have done that you felt would cause my destruction, because it made me the great person I am today. Thanks for your help and much love.

All the Sorors of *Alpha Kappa Alpha Sorority Inc., Sigma Alpha Omega Chapter* (please forgive me for leaving during my dark season, I will be back really soon now. I love you all.)

Warm loving thanks to:

Auntie Prophetess Barbara Brown (You prayed when I could not, and I thank you.)

Pastor Marsha Buford (Thanks for modeling what a true woman of God looks like.)

Apostle W.B. Jefferson (Thanks for being a loving mother to me, and changing my name.)

Minister Janet Lamar (There is no distance in my love for you.)

Katanna Harden (You will always be my sister.)

Karen Williams-Cooper (my sister/friend)

Claudia Palmer (Keeper of all my secrets.)

Tyrone Johnson (Cousin, your testimony saved my life.)

Ronald Heyward (Thank you for feeding me everyday when I could not afford to pay. And thanks for believing in me.)

Pamela Green-Jackson (Girl, thank you for supporting me.)

Anne Roise (Thanks for always encouraging me into greatness.)

RayShon Murdock-Williams (Skee-wee baby! It's never too late in life to find a true friend.)

Melissa Hargabrook (Thank you for being my sister from the very beginning, my constant friend, and giving me love even when I didn't feel worth loving.)

Libby Mills (Thank you for sharing your testimony with me in my time of weakness, and for editing the book.)

Special, Special thanks:

Tyra Banks (During my 78 days of depression, I watched America's Next Top Model all day every weekend, and Tuesday, and at the end of it all I found that I was beautiful, and that there is a "top model" in all of us. Thank you for helping me realize that.)

To contact this author: offthefloor.mlb@gmail.com

Thanks to my daughter Andrea for making my
40th birthday so special with your poem:

Beauty Never Fades

Before you even knew it, you were a beacon of beauty.
    Since no one let you know this, I've made it my duty.

You look in the mirror and see only part of who you are
    But when I look at you I see a beauty that runs far.

No matter how long it took you to realize.
    You've always been beautiful in my eyes.

With people like you birthdays really shouldn't matter,
    Because you're beautiful now, and will be in the latter.

Shh speak lowly, don't give everyone a surprise,
    Because today you're 40 and don't look a bit over 25.

No one knows, or has seen your beauty mature.
    But I know, and I've seen your beauty endure.

When people see you now they say "WOW she's hot"
    But I know you're steamin hot whether you're 170 or not.

God told you that one day you were to inspire many.
    And you started in '93, you've inspired me plenty.

I love taking pictures, but not just to see the beauty in me
    I take them to show you the beauty in you that I see.

For along time you thought your body had never seen true beauty.
    You've taken the childish comments calling you Big Booty Judy.

You've learned from AKA that "Pretty Girls Wear 20 Pearls"
    But what jewel do we give to the 8th wonder of the world?

I just wanted you to know that your pretty will go away.
    But don't fret mommy 'cause

              TRUE BEAUTY NEVER FADES.

                    -Andrea' Perry